FOREWORD

FOR the past few years, the Foundation has been engaged on studies in school organization, and its attention has focussed in particular on methods of grouping. This area has become the scene of lively discussions: understandably so, since differing methods of allocation to classes (and to groups within classes) reflect widely differing educational philosophies. The decision to stream, or not to stream, will spring in the main from the head teacher's view of the aims and objectives of his school and his beliefs about the abilities and capabilities of his pupils. Since the genesis of such decisions is complex, it follows that research in this field cannot be simple. And no-one, it is hoped, expects research to 'prove' that one method of organization is 'right', another one 'wrong'. What it can do, of course, is to attempt to show the effects that are likely to flow from a particular form of organization, and to contrast these with the different pattern of effect that ensues from a different organizational method.

This present report is a side-shoot from our main research on streaming. It attacks a problem which is a very real one: the problem of organizing a junior school when the numbers are so small that a 'tidy' division into classes to fit the four-year age-range is impossible. The difficulties are most obvious with 2-class and 3-class schools, but they can also be intractable with 5-class schools—and with 4-class when the numbers in age-groups are disparate. The report studies the differences produced by the two common attempts at solution: 'according to age', and 'traditional standard'. It will, I believe, be welcomed by teachers and head teachers who are faced with such problems, for the practical help which it offers. But it has, too, a wider significance and a relevance to the major grouping controversy.

I, personally, found the report quite fascinating for the way in which it harked back—unwittingly—to problems and controversies engaging teachers forty years ago, when the elementary school switched from grouping by 'standards' to grouping by age. How useful a research of this kind would have been in the twenties! The teaching profession was then faced with an organizational change of much greater severity than anything it has since experienced (including 'going comprehensive'), and yet it was achieved with little complaint and with what may reasonably be regarded as astonishing success. Few have ever given the teachers adequate recognition of this achievement: as one whose first job was in an elementary school during the later period of adaptation I have never underrated the difficulties—or the success. And this report reiterates, with authority, so many of the points that we, in a totally subjective way, had come to appreciate. It supports, too, similar experience in countries such as the USA where organization is by grades: 'If you are allowed only one method of locating the highest IQ in a classroom, your chance of getting the right child is better if you merely look in the class register and take the youngest than if you trust the teacher's judgement' (WITTY, P. ed., *The Gifted Child*, 1951, D. C. Heath). The present report underlines again the teacher's difficulty of making adequate allowance for age when judging the ability of children.

The authors are to be congratulated on producing a report that not only adds to our knowledge in the general field of grouping and streaming, but also offers practical and factual data which will be of the greatest assistance to those working in small junior schools.

STEPHEN WISEMAN

December 1968

CONTENTS

PART I

A Comparison of 'Traditional Standard' and 'According to Age' Schools

PART II

The Mixed-Age Class

LIST OF TABLES

ACKNOWLEDGEMENTS

We should like to thank all the heads and teachers who co-operated in this study. Also thanks are due to Miss J. Tarryer, Miss E. Rendell and Miss J. Mason, who carried out the tabulation and statistical analysis, and to Miss B. Bailey and Miss E. Hendry who gave valuable assistance in the reporting of the data.

JANET BOURI and JOAN BARKER LUNN

Research Design

1.1 Introduction

The National Foundation for Educational Research was asked by the Department of Education and Science to undertake a study into the effects of different forms of grouping in small junior schools.[1] This was planned as a complement to research already under way at the Foundation, which was examining the effects of 'Streaming' and other forms of grouping in large junior schools.

1.2 The Background to the Study

The first phase of the 'Streaming' research was a survey of general practices, reported to the Plowden Committee in April 1965. This was undertaken with two aims: (a) to establish the incidence of 'Streaming' and the methods of organization practised in junior schools, and (b) to obtain further information needed for the selection of a sample of schools for further study.

This initial survey had shown that, whereas schools with less than eight classes were not able to 'stream' in the classical sense, i.e. to divide each year-group into at least an A- and B-stream, certain forms of organization did nevertheless exist within them that exemplified the dichotomy between homogeneous and heterogeneous ability grouping.

The organizations typified in the Survey Report[2] as (a) *According to Age* and (b) *Traditional Standard* occur widely in schools with less than

---

[1] Small schools have been defined as schools having four or less junior classes (58 per cent of junior schools or departments are of this size and account for 26 per cent of the junior school population). For the purposes of this study, 'middle-sized' schools of five classes were also included.

[2] BARKER LUNN, J. C. (1967). 'The effects of streaming and other forms of grouping in junior schools: Interim report', *New Research in Education*, vol. 1, pp. 4-45. (Distributed by NFER).

eight classes, and were thought to merit further investigation, in addition to the more detailed work on large schools. For ease of reference, these two types of organization are defined once more in the terms of the Survey Report.

1.3 Types of Organization in Small Junior Schools

1. 'ACCORDING TO AGE'

This type of organization is a form of heterogeneous ability grouping. It occurs when pupils are assigned to classes on the basis of age, without reference to attainment or ability. It will be seen that, in schools with more than four classes, such grouping may give classes containing less than the full span of a year-group, whereas in smaller schools, classes must contain a full year-group or more. The practical implications of this system will therefore vary widely according to the size of the school in question. For example, a two-class school grouped *According to Age* might have pupils from the first and second years in one class, and the third- and fourth-year children in another. In a school with three classes, as in the diagram below, breaks *within* year-groups will have to be made to form classes, as there are still fewer classes than year-groups.

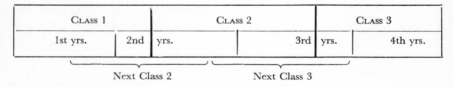

The continual re-forming of classes which a system such as this entails, means that pupils might annually experience a fairly major change of classmates, and it is unlikely that any class will proceed through the schools as a unit. It also means that in schools where there are fewer than four classes, pupils will spend two years in the same class at least once.

2. 'TRADITIONAL STANDARD'

This form of homogeneous ability grouping is found mostly in small schools, i.e. those of less than five classes, and seems to be a partial survival of the old system of 'standards'. It involves retention or acceleration of pupils, while tending to produce a wider age-range within the class. The *Traditional Standard* form of organization has something in common with the 'grade' system found in the USA and on the Continent.

A strictly enforced 'grade' system usually upgrades through achievement only; so that, at the end of the school year, promotion is decided according to how much the pupil is judged to have learned. If he has apparently absorbed the work of one grade, he moves on to the next; but if he has not, he repeats the grade for the next period or year. Theoretically a very slow learner or dull child could spend his school days in Grade I. In most grade systems, however, age is taken into account. The amount to which it is taken into account varies greatly from one country to another.

The survey of general practices showed that in schools using the *Traditional Standard* method, the most common type of class was composed of average children plus a few bright younger pupils (33 per cent of the classes were of this type). The next most frequent were classes in which a few less able children were kept down with a class of average younger children (30 per cent). It was, however, not uncommon to find a combination of these characteristics in the same class: 24 per cent of the classes were composed of brighter, younger, and duller, older children, joined with a 'middle-aged' average group. In such a case, three year-groups would be represented in the one class.

The survey revealed, on the basis of approximately 1,000 'small' schools—i.e. schools having four classes or less—that homogeneous and heterogeneous ability grouping, as represented by *Traditional Standard* and *According to Age* methods of organization, were equally popular: in fact, 70 per cent of small schools used one or other of these methods. Twenty per cent of small schools had only one junior class, which meant that these schools had no choice of method, and the remaining 10 per cent used neither the *Traditional Standard* nor *According to Age* forms of groupings, but some 'other method'.

There are four year-groups in the junior school and a problem of the small school with three, two, five or even four classes, if the number of pupils in the different year-groups is not equal, is how to accommodate or allocate pupils to classes. In most small schools, year-groups have to be split in order to achieve an approximately equal number of children in each class. In doing this the head may use either *age* or *achievement* as his criterion for assignment to classes. Using the former criterion, the head would allocate children to classes strictly on the basis of age in months and when one class was full, would allocate pupils to the next and so on. Using achievement as the criterion, as in the *Traditional Standard* method, the problem of splitting a year-group would be solved by 'putting up' the brightest of a year-group and/or keeping the dullest of a year-group back with a class of younger children.

However, in some cases, the head in the *Traditional Standard* school promotes and demotes pupils when he has not been forced by circumstances to split a year-group, or keeps duller pupils back, enabling younger, brighter pupils to be in a class of older pupils. When this

3

occurs it has been referred to in the text as 'pure promotion' or 'pure demotion' in contrast to 'split promotion' or 'split demotion'.

The choice of *Traditional Standard* or *According to Age* methods seems to be associated with the number of junior classes in the schools. There is a tendency for schools with four or two junior classes to adopt the *According to Age* method, whereas three-class schools tend to favour the *Traditional Standard* method.[1]

1.4 The Aims of the Small Schools Study

In the light of the findings reviewed above, the Department of Education and Science asked the National Foundation to undertake a second cross-sectional[2] study of the organization of smaller junior schools, which is the subject of the present report.

The objectives of the study can be outlined as follows:

1. To compare small junior schools organized by *Traditional Standard* and *According to Age* methods, in respect of (a) performance on attainment tests, (b) the degree of homogeneity in terms of attainment, and (c) certain social characteristics of their pupils as reflected in questionnaire data.

2. To examine the problems of classes with pupils drawn from mixed year-groups, with regard to (a) the teaching methods and grouping practices used by their teachers, (b) the relationship between these practices and pupils' attainments, (c) the teachers' awareness of 'age-spread' in mixed-age classes as regards their expectations of mature behaviour and their allowance for age when rating ability, (d) the friendship patterns of pupils in mixed-age classes, and (e) the examination of children in a minority away from their year-group, with particular reference to their socialization and levels of attainment, and to the particular effects of 'promotion' and 'demotion'.

3. To analyse the comparative attainments of pupils in large versus small junior schools.

1.5 The Sample

Approximately 500 small schools, which seemed to employ one of the two types of grouping mentioned above, were chosen from the 2,000 schools for which data were available. A fact-finding questionnaire was sent to these schools to obtain information about the way in which classes were formed, as a check to the data obtained in

---

[1,2] BARKER LUNN, J. C. (1967). 'The effects of streaming and other forms of grouping in junior schools: Interim report', *New Research in Education*, vol. 1, pp. 4-45. (Distributed by NFER).

the survey two years earlier.   Following this, an attempt was made to select matched pairs of schools, in which one school organized its classes *According to Age* while the other adopted a *Traditional Standard* organization.

Small schools tend to be Junior Mixed with Infants situated in urban and rural areas.   Roughly half are non-denominational and half are Church of England schools.[1]

Schools were initially matched on the following criteria:

1. Denomination, i.e. Church of England or non-denominational.
2. Type of school and locality, i.e. Junior rural; Junior and Infant/rural; Junior/urban; and Junior and Infant/urban.
3. Number of classes in the school.
4. Geographical region (North, Midlands or South of England).
5. Predominant socio-economic status of parents.
6. Percentage of children in the LEA attending non-selective schools.

A second questionnaire was sent to the provisionally selected schools, to obtain information applicable to the 1964-5 school year.   Finally, on the basis of this information, 36 schools or 18 matched pairs, were selected in what was hoped would be a final sample.

Unfortunately, the analysis of test and questionnaire data revealed changes in school organization and other unforeseen characteristics which disrupted several matched pairs and prevented four pairs of schools from being used in the analysis.   Thus the sample was reduced to 28 schools: 14 *Traditional Standard* and 14 *According to Age*.   Ninety-four teachers and 2,822 junior pupils were involved in the Small Schools study.   Details of the sample are given in Table 1.

As can be seen from Table 1, the two halves of the sample matched satisfactorily on nine out of ten criteria initially applied to them.   The exception consisted of the percentages falling into each category of

TABLE 1: *The 'Traditional Standard'/'According to Age' Sample*

	1	2	3			4	5				
			SIZE OF SCHOOL			AVERAGE SIZE OF CLASS	SOCIAL CLASS PERCENTAGE† (Father's occupation)				
	No. OF SCHOOLS	No. OF CLASSES	2— *class*	3— *class*	4/5— *class*		1	2	3	4	5
TS	14	47	4	3	7	32·9	5%	8%	38%	32%	16%
AA	14	47	3	3	8	31·7	6%	10%	32%	32%	19%

continued

[1] BARKER LUNN, J. C. (1967).   'The effects of streaming and other forms of grouping in junior schools: Interim report', *New Research in Education*, vol. 1, pp. 4-45. (Distributed by NFER).

	6	7			8		9		10	
	AV. NO. ON ROLL (JNRS.)	GEOGRAPHICAL REGION			TYPE OF AREA		DENOMI- NATION		LEA's SELECTION PROCEDURE	
		South	Midlands	North	Urban	Rural	C of E	ND	More than 70% Secondary Modern	Less than 70% Secondary Modern
TS	102·6	8	2	4	6	8	7	7	11	3
AA	99·0	6	2	6	6	8	7	7	10	4

†**Note:** Teachers were asked to indicate each pupil's father's occupation according to the following categories of the Registrar General's classification: 1 = Professional/Managerial; 2 = Clerical/Supervisory; 3 = Skilled workers; 4 = Semi-skilled workers; 5 = Unskilled workers.

father's occupation: it can be seen that the 'spread' of social class is greater in the *According to Age* schools, while the majority (70 per cent) of pupils in the *Traditional Standard* schools came from families in social classes 3 or 4. To help overcome this weakness of match, all comparisons involving social class have been made on the basis of two separate groupings, i.e. of class 1, 2 and 3 pupils into an 'upper' group and of class 4 and 5 pupils into one categorized as 'lower'.

1.6 **Procedure**

As this piece of research was intended to complement the study of the effects of streaming and non-streaming being carried out by the NFER, the same or similar questionnaires and the same tests were used.[1] Testing was carried out in June 1965.

The following questionnaires and tests were used:

1. A Teacher Personal Data questionnaire, to give information on sex, age, experience as a teacher, etc.
2. A Class Teacher questionnaire, asking for information on class facilities, frequency of 'traditional' and 'progressive' type lessons and grouping within the class.
3. A Pupil Assessment questionnaire, asking for information on pupils' ages, social class (father's occupation), behaviour (rated on six criteria), and level of achievement.
4. Tests in Reading (SRA) and English (SEA).
5. Tests in Mechanical Arithmetic (SMA), Problem Arithmetic (SPA) and Number Concept (SCA).

[1] BARKER LUNN, J. C. (1967). 'The effects of streaming and non-streaming in junior schools: Second interim report', *New Research in Education*, vol. 1, pp. 46-75. (Distributed by NFER).

6. Ability tests—verbal and non-verbal.
7. A specially constructed sociomatrix (See page 25 for further details).

The tests and questionnaires were marked and coded, and the data obtained were submitted to machine analysis in accordance with the aims and hypotheses of the study.

PART I

*A Comparison of 'Traditional Standard'
and 'According to Age' Schools*

SECTION TWO

The Characteristics and Attitudes of Teachers in 'Traditional Standard' and 'According to Age' Schools

2.1 Introduction

In the report on 'The effects of streaming and non-streaming in junior schools: Second interim report', *New Research in Education*, Vol. I, 1967, mention was made of the importance and effect of teachers' experience, attitudes and practices on the attainments of their pupils. First, therefore, a comparison was made of these characteristics in the two types of school:

    (a) The age and experience of their teachers,

    (b) The incidence of 'traditional' and 'progressive' type lessons,

    (c) Seating arrangements and grouping practices for English, Reading and Arithmetic, and

    (d) The classroom facilities available in the two types of school.

2.2 Age and Experience of Teachers

No significant differences occurred regarding the age of teachers and the amount of their teaching experience. There was no tendency for either of these types of school to attract either very young teachers or those nearing retirement, as is shown by the following table:

TABLE 2: *Age of Teachers in 'Traditional Standard'/'According to Age' Schools*

	UNDER 25	25–30	31–35	36–45	46–55	56–65	TOTAL
Traditional Standard Schools	3	8	4	17	12	3	47
According to Age Schools	6	6	4	18	7	6	47

2.3 The Incidence of 'Traditional' and 'Progressive' Type Lessons

There were also no significant differences between the two types of school in the degree to which 'traditional' and 'progressive' type lessons were given (for details of these scales, see Report[1]). This is not surprising in view of the relationship known to exist between scores on these scales and the ages of the teachers completing them,[2] i.e. that younger teachers tend to employ 'progressive' methods of teaching more frequently than their older colleagues.

2.4 Seating Arrangements and Grouping Practices

A comparison of seating arrangements showed no significant differences. In both types of school, pupils tended to be streamed at least for part if not for all of the time (see Table 3). (For further details, see para. 7.3.)

TABLE 3: *Seating Arrangement in the Class*

	STREAMED FOR MOST OR ALL OF THE TIME	STREAMED PART OF THE TIME	COMPLETE FREE CHOICE	TOTAL	REJECTS
Traditional Standard	13	15	8	36	11
According to Age	12	20	8	40	7
Total	25	35	16	76	18

Similarly there were only slight differences in the grouping practices employed in the two types of school in the teaching of English, Reading and Problem Arithmetic (see Tables 4, 5, 6).

TABLE 4: *Grouping Practices for English*

	TAUGHT AS A CLASS	GROUPS OF MIXED ABILITY	GROUPS OF SIMILAR ABILITY	TAUGHT INDIVI- DUALLY	BY A COM- BINATION OF METHODS	TOTAL	REJECTS
Traditional Standard	13	1	12	6	15	47	
According to Age	16	5	10	3	12	46	1
Total	29	6	22	9	27	93	1

[1,2] BARKER LUNN, J. C. (1967). 'The effects of streaming and non-streaming in junior schools: Second interim report', *New Research in Education*, vol. 1, pp. 46-75. (Distributed by NFER).

TABLE 5: *Grouping Practices for Reading*

	TAUGHT AS A CLASS	GROUPS OF MIXED ABILITY	GROUPS OF SIMILAR ABILITY	TAUGHT INDIVI- DUALLY	BY A COM- BINATION OF METHODS	TOTAL	REJECTS
Traditional Standard	2	1	12	17	5	37	10
According to Age	0	4	17	9	14	44	3
Total	2	5	29	26	19	81	13

TABLE 6: *Grouping Practices for Arithmetic*

	TAUGHT AS A CLASS	GROUPS OF MIXED ABILITY	GROUPS OF SIMILAR ABILITY	TAUGHT INDIVI- DUALLY	BY A COM- BINATION OF METHODS	TOTAL	REJECTS
Traditional Standard	2	2	19	14	10	47	
According to Age	2	1	24	9	10	46	1
Total	4	3	43	23	20	93	1

There was also no significant difference between the two types of school in their score for classroom facilities. This was based on a composite 'facilities' score (good lighting, new desks, outside distractions, classroom space).

It is therefore apparent that, while the two halves of the sample differed radically in the approach of heads to problems of organization (presumably stemming to some extent from differences in educational philosophy), these differences did not apply to several of those variables which would have most effect on the children. In the case of larger 'streamed' and 'non-streamed' schools, differences of age of staff and teaching methods have been found to relate very meaningfully to the type of organization, but this is obviously not the case in the small schools under review.

It must be remembered that, although *Traditional Standard* and *According to Age* methods of organization are examples of homogeneous and heterogeneous ability grouping respectively, they cannot be regarded as being the equivalent of 'streamed' and 'non-streamed' organizations in the small school. 'Non-streamed' schools are still a comparative rarity (about 11 per cent of all large junior schools) and they tend to be staffed by teachers who are also in a minority in terms of their views and opinions on teaching methods and other educational matters.[1]   On the other hand, *According to Age* and *Traditional Standard* schools each account for 35 per cent of small schools, and it is thus not to be expected that the staff of either will consist of teachers holding minority, extreme views.

Also, the problems of organization facing the heads of small schools with fewer classes than year-groups are radically different from those confronting the head of a large school.   The head of a large school, say a three-stream or 'three classes per year-group' school, has to decide whether to allocate pupils to classes on the basis of perceived ability (i.e. to stream) or whether deliberately to form classes which are heterogeneous as regards ability.   It would be unwise to assume that the educational philosophies of a *Traditional Standard* and an *According to Age* head are necessarily the same as those held by the typical 'streamed' and typical 'non-streamed' heads.

---

[1] BARKER LUNN, J. C. (1967).   'The effects of streaming and other forms of grouping in junior schools: Interim report', *New Research in Education*, vol. 1, pp. 4-45.   (Distributed by NFER).

SECTION THREE

Pupils' Attainments in Relation to Size of School

3.1 Introduction

The NFER Survey Report[1] suggested that pupils from small schools might find themselves at an academic disadvantage compared with their contemporaries in larger schools. Seventy-six per cent of classes in small schools were composed of two or more year-groups; year-groups were split, children being separated when they were 'younger', 'older', 'brighter' or 'slower' than the majority.

For all administrative purposes, children in a year-group are regarded as the same age—they take the 11 + at the same time and leave the junior school at the same time. Children finding themselves in a class composed mainly of children of a younger year-group may miss the verbal stimulus of their own year-group; also, class lessons will presumably be geared to younger children. The 'moving up' of the older, or brighter children in a year-group, into a class consisting mainly of children a year older, may give rise to similar problems.

As a check upon the comparative levels of attainment found in schools of different sizes, the performances of second- and third-year pupils on the Reading and Problem Arithmetic tests were considered.

3.2 Caution

It must be pointed out that the sample of large schools was not representative. The only data available on large schools were those obtained in the course of the Foundation's survey into the 'Effects of streaming and non-streaming in junior schools', which was a study of fifty streamed and fifty non-streamed schools. As it was pointed out

[1] BARKER LUNN, J. C. (1967). 'The effects of streaming and other forms of grouping in junior schools: Interim report', *New Research in Education*, vol. 1, pp. 4-45. (Distributed by NFER)

in the previous section, non-streamed schools are in the minority (11 per cent of large schools use non-streaming) and 50 per cent of them would obviously be an over-representation in any sample of large schools. Thus it was decided first to compare the achievements of all the large schools with small schools; and secondly, to compare only the streamed schools—probably representing three-quarters or more of the large schools' policies and views—with those of the small school.

3.3 Large v. Small Schools

Comparisons were made between large and small junior schools in the means and standard deviations of the scores of their third-year pupils on the Reading and Problem Arithmetic tests, holding the social class and urban/rural factors constant. (Separate comparisons were carried out for three social class groups: classes 1 and 2; class 3; classes 4 and 5—see footnote to Table 1, page 6.)

3.4 Mean Performance in Urban Small Schools v. Large Schools

No significant difference emerged for the Reading test. On the Problem Arithmetic test, pupils in urban small schools obtained higher mean scores which were significantly better than the scores of pupils in large schools.

In order to obviate any error arising from the fact that the children in small schools were approximately one month older when the tests were administered, an estimated average difference in the score attributable to one month was calculated for each test, and the observed differences were adjusted accordingly. The adjustment to the standard error of difference proved to be negligible, and adjusted differences were still slightly significant in favour of small schools ($P < \cdot 05$) for Problem Arithmetic, in all except the middle-class group (classes 1 and 2). Adjustments were also made for the Reading test but the differences between urban large and small schools were still non-significant.

3.5 Mean Performance in Urban Small Schools v. Large Streamed Schools

When the results of the urban small schools were compared with the streamed schools only, there were no statistically significant differences on the Reading or the Problem Arithmetic test.

3.6 Mean Performance in Small Urban Schools v. Small Rural Schools

A comparison was also made between urban and rural small schools. Again, no significant difference emerged for the Reading test. The only difference which did reach significance was that of the Problem Arithmetic test of the lowest socio-economic group (classes 4 and 5), where urban school results were higher than those for rural school children $(P < \cdot 05)$.

3.7 **Conclusions**

1. There is no evidence that small urban schools differ from small rural schools in performance at Reading and Problem Arithmetic.

2. It would seem that pupils in small schools do not fare any worse in terms of achievement than pupils in large schools. However, this conclusion must be tentative for the reason stated under paragraph 3.2.

A Comparison of Pupils' Attainments in 'Traditional Standard' and 'According to Age' Schools

4.1 Introduction

Does either form of school organization produce better achievement results? Does the spread of scores differ for pupils from schools adopting different forms of organization? Advocates of homogeneous class grouping would claim that by placing the individual pupil with others of a similar attainment level (even where this entails 'promotion' or 'demotion' away from his own year-group) he has a greater opportunity to develop his capabilities to the maximum.

4.2 Procedure

In order to assess attainments in the two types of school, tests of Reading, English, Mechanical and Problem Arithmetic were given to all four junior year-groups. These tests were devised to be suitable for all ages from 7-plus to 10-plus and all children completed the same test. In addition, a Concept Arithmetic and a Verbal reasoning test were given to all except the first-year children; the fourth-year children were also given a test of Non-Verbal reasoning. In all, seven tests (see para. 1.6) were administered:

(a) Reading: 7 +, 8 +, 9 + and 10 + pupils

(b) English: 7 +, 8 +, 9 + and 10 + pupils

(c) Mechanical Arithmetic: 7 +, 8 +, 9 + and 10 + pupils

(d) Problem Arithmetic: 7 +, 8 +, 9 + and 10 + pupils

(e) Primary Verbal: 8 + 9 + and 10 + pupils

(f) Concept Arithmetic: 8 +, 9 + and 10 + pupils

(g) Verbal/Non-Verbal: 10 + pupils only.

Tests of significance were applied to results from the two types of school organization in terms of
  (a) differences between the mean performances on tests, and
  (b) differences between the standard deviations of the scores on the tests.

4.3 Differences in Average Performances

The results of the attainment tests showed that where differences between mean scores were significant, the difference was in favour of pupils in *According to Age* schools. Furthermore, even where the differences did not reach statistical significance, the trend was to superior performance in the *According to Age* schools. Table A in the Appendix sets out statistically significant differences in mean scores on the individual tests achieved by pupils of *Traditional Standard* and *According to Age* schools. Two hundred-and-sixteen comparisons of mean test scores were made: of these, 62 were statistically significant and favoured the *According to Age* schools. Another 115 favoured the *According to Age*, but the difference in these mean scores did not reach statistical significance (see Appendix).

On some of the tests, there was no doubt about the superiority of the pupils in *According to Age* schools, and on others there was very little difference between the two schools. On the English, Primary Verbal and Verbal tests, for example, the children in *According to Age* schools did particularly well and at no point did pupils in *Traditional Standard* schools do better. On the Reading, Non-Verbal and Problem Arithmetic tests the trend was also very much in favour of *According to Age* schools.

However, on the Mechanical and Concept Arithmetic tests no clear pattern emerged and none of the comparisons between mean scores for the two types of school was significant.

The tests which showed the most consistent superiority of pupils from *According to Age* schools were those measuring to some degree verbal facility or comprehension: Reading, English, Primary Verbal and Verbal tests. In fact, the tests giving the greatest superiority for *According to Age* pupils were those which would seem to deal to a greater extent with material relevant to the child's everyday social interactions and experiences, rather than with activities more restricted to the context of formal learning within the classroom. This would certainly seem to be true of the Reading and Verbal tests, and to a lesser extent with the English test. Having already established that there were no significant differences between teachers in *Traditional Standard* and *According to Age* schools, these facts lend support to the suggestion that differences in achievement between *According to Age* and *Traditional Standard* pupils are attributable directly to the effects of organizational factors.

4.4 **Differences in the Standard Deviations** (i.e. spread of scores obtained)

Comparisons were made of the overall distribution of the test scores obtained by pupils from *Traditional Standard* and *According to Age* schools. Results, where significant, indicated a narrower range of performance in *According to Age* schools. Table B in the Appendix to this report sets out the details of these comparisons.

As with the mean scores, the difference in standard deviation between the two types of school was particularly evident in tests where emphasis was principally on verbal dexterity or comprehension. No significant differences emerged on the Problem Arithmetic test, and only a few subgroups differed on the Concept Arithmetic and Mechanical Arithmetic tests.

One of the interesting findings here was that the greatest number of statistically significant differences in spread of scores (i.e. in the standard deviations) occurred within the 10-plus age-group. This would suggest that the spread of attainments increases, in the *Traditional Standard* school, as the children move up the school. In other words, the gap between the attainment scores of the brightest and dullest children at 7-plus is more or less the same in the two types of school, but at 10-plus, the gap is wider in the *Traditional Standard* than in the *According to Age* school. Thus it would appear from this cross-sectional study that as a result of the school organization, pupils' attainments in *Traditional Standard* schools become more heterogeneous, rather than homogeneous, and that there is an increasing diversity of performance as pupils proceed up the school. In order to throw more light on this, let us examine the achievements of the least able (i.e. the bottom quartile) and the most able pupils (i.e. the top quartile) in the two types of school.

Proportions of Children Scoring High and Low Marks

As a check upon the proportion of children in each type of school scoring high or low marks, the upper and lower quartiles were calculated for each of those tests in which the mean scores had been significantly different.

Results indicated that, on all tests except for Reading, at 10-plus (which was non-significant), the *According to Age* school quartiles were higher than the *Traditional Standard* quartiles. In other words, the bottom 25 per cent and the top 25 per cent of *According to Age* pupils reached a higher level than did their *Traditional Standard* equivalents. These differences reached statistical significance for the lower quartiles, in virtually all cases, and for several of the tests, up to the age of 9-plus, for the upper quartile. This can be seen from Table 7.

TABLE 7A: *Test Scores obtained by the Bottom Quartile in 'Traditional Standard' and 'According to Age' Schools*

Test	Age	TRADITIONAL STANDARD			ACCORDING TO AGE			SIGNIFICANCE OF DIFFERENCES	
		N	*Bottom Quartile*	*Error Variance*	*N*	*Bottom Quartile*	*Error Variance*	*Standard Error*	*Significance Level†*
Reading	7+	325	8·6	·48	335	12·0	·38	·93	0·1%
	8+	313	14·2	·58	320	16·0	·46	1·02	NS
	9+	348	20·3	·53	295	22·4	·47	1·00	5%
	10+	335	25·6	·58	315	27·6	·34	·96	5%
English	7+	334	2·9	·80	338	6·1	·87	1·3	5%
	8+	318	8·3	1·47	322	13·0	1·56	1·7	1%
	9+	349	17·5	1·65	291	25·1	1·75	1·84	0·1%
	10+	325	28·3	1·69	305	37·6	1·17	1·69	0·1%
Primary Verbal	8+	312	22·5	2·68	314	29·8	2·45	2·27	1%
	9+	344	40·8	2·46	298	47·8	2·05	2·12	1%
	10+	328	54·5	2·19	306	59·5	1·42	1·90	1%
Verbal	10+	326	13·6	·51	303	18·9	·44	·98	0·1%

TABLE 7B: *Test Scores obtained by the Top Quartile in 'Traditional Standard' and 'According to Age' Schools*

Test	Age	TRADITIONAL STANDARD			ACCORDING TO AGE			SIGNIFICANCE OF DIFFERENCES	
		N	*Top Quartile*	*Error Variance*	*N*	*Top Quartile*	*Error Variance*	*Standard Error*	*Significance Level†*
Reading	7+	325	22·6	·48	335	23·0	·38	·93	NS
	8+	313	28·5	·58	320	29·2	·46	1·02	NS
	9+	348	34·4	·53	295	34·7	·47	1·00	NS
	10+	335	38·6	·58	315	37·6	·34	·96	NS
English	7+	334	19·3	·80	338	25·2	·87	1·3	0·1%
	8+	318	33·8	1·47	322	40·9	1·56	1·7	0·1%
	9+	349	46·9	1·65	291	51·2	1·75	1·84	5%
	10+	325	53·1	1·69	305	56·2	1·17	1·69	NS
Primary Verbal	8+	312	58·6	2·68	314	63·5	2·45	2·27	5%
	9+	344	72·0	2·46	298	72·9	2·05	2·12	NS
	10+	328	77·3	2·19	306	78·1	1·42	1·90	NS
Verbal	10+	326	30·0	·51	303	31·2	·44	·98	NS

† *Comment:* In all cases where differences reached statistical significance, *According to Age* quartiles were higher than those obtained by *Traditional Standard* pupils. In all cases, except for the Reading test at 10+, the quartile figures confirm the trend for the *According to Age* quartiles to be higher than those of *Traditional Standard* schools.

Graph I below illustrates the differences between the two types of school in the mean scores, and in the different proportions of pupils scoring low marks (in this case on the English test at 10-plus).

From the graph, it can be seen that 20 per cent of the children in the *Traditional Standard* schools as against only 8 per cent in the *According to Age* scored less than 20 marks. The graph below shows that the mean score for all schools was 42·40; and that, whereas 50 per cent of the *Traditional Standard* pupils scored below this, only 35 per cent of the *According to Age* pupils did so.

GRAPH I: *Cumulative Distribution Curve of 10 + Pupils' Scores on English Test*

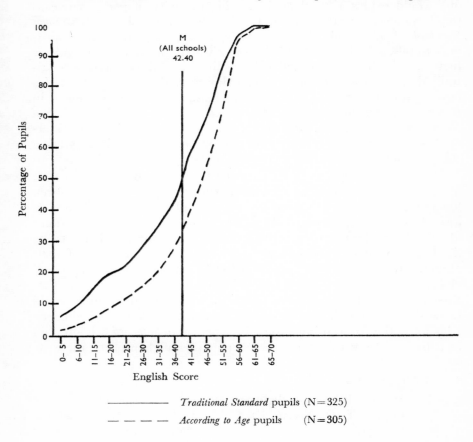

—————— *Traditional Standard* pupils (N=325)

— — — — *According to Age* pupils   (N=305)

Thus it would appear that where pupils are placed in classes in terms of their age rather than their perceived ability or level of attainment, slower pupils benefit, and this benefit, far from being achieved at the expense of 'slowing down' the brighter elements in their year-group, may be shared by more gifted pupils too. In contrast, the less academically gifted children in *Traditional Standard* schools, who ran the risk of finding themselves separated from their own year-group, achieved consistently lower scores, whilst their brighter contemporaries appeared not to reap any scholastic benefit from being promoted away from their year-group.

Since no significant differences were found between the teaching of the two types of school, in terms of the incidence of 'traditional' or 'progressive' type lessons—both variables found in previous studies to bear a relation to pupils' achievements—the difference in spread of achievement scores would seem to be largely attributable to the method of organization adopted by the two types of school. If this is so, one would expect to find an increasing diversity of performance as pupils proceed up the school, i.e. fourth-year pupils in *Traditional Standard* schools should show a wider span of achievement than third-year pupils, who in turn should have a wider spread than second- or first-year children. In order to ascertain this with certainty a longitudinal study would be necessary. However, the indications of this cross-sectional study are that, with increasing age, the differences in range of performance between *According to Age* and *Traditional Standard* schools tend to become increasingly pronounced, and that this difference is chiefly a function of the different proportions of children scoring relatively low marks on the achievement tests.

The question arises as to how far the larger number of low scorers in the *Traditional Standard* schools represent pupils who have been 'demoted' because of perceived low ability and who are now in a class away from their age-group. As will be shown in subsequent sections, 'demoted' children tend to exhibit more behaviour problems, to be liked less by their teachers and to be under-rated in terms of their ability. It would not be unreasonable to suppose that a 'demoted' child would conform to his teacher's low expectations of him, and that these factors contribute to poor progress. A longitudinal study would be needed to establish whether or not it is in fact the 'demoted' children who form the low-scoring group in *Traditional Standard* schools, but facts derived from this study suggest that this might well be the case.

4.5 Conclusions

1. Where differences between the mean scores obtained by pupils of *Traditional Standard* and *According to Age* schools reached statistical significance, these were in favour of *According to Age* schools.

2. *According to Age* schools achieved a greater degree of homogeneity in their pupils' achievements, i.e. a narrower spread of score.

3. The superiority of *According to Age* schools would seem to derive primarily from a lower proportion of their pupils obtaining lower than average scores. There was also evidence to suggest that the *According to Age* form of school organization may also produce a higher proportion of high scorers on the tests.

The Social Experience of Pupils in 'Traditional Standard' and 'According to Age' Schools

5.1 Overall Comparisons of Children in 'Traditional Standard' and 'According to Age' Schools in terms of Maladjustment Ratings

The teachers of all classes taking part in this study completed a 'Pupil Assessment' questionnaire, in which they were asked to rate each pupil in their class, on a four-point scale, on the following statements of behaviour:

(a) 'This pupil gets into fights or bullies other children'.
(b) 'This pupil is "picked on", teased and baited by other children'.
(c) 'This pupil is withdrawn, and plays and talks very little with other children'.
(d) 'This pupil is a pleasure to have in the class'.

The teachers were asked to say whether each statement, as applied to each pupil, was true: (1) 'most of the time', (2) 'quite often', (3) 'sometimes', or (4) 'seldom or never'.[1]

Comparisons were made of the ratings of pupils in *Traditional Standard* and *According to Age* schools, both overall, and also in terms of social class (classes 1, 2 and 3 being combined to form an upper socio-economic group, and classes 4 and 5 to form a lower socio-economic group).[2]

For both social groups there was a significant tendency for *Traditional Standard* pupils to be more prone to fights than were children in schools

---

[1] For the purpose of analysis a pupil was rated as prone to fighting, withdrawn, disobedient or teased if any of these characteristics were attributed to him (or her) 'sometimes', 'quite often' or 'most of the time'. A pupil was considered 'unpleasurable' if he was *not* rated as 'pleasurable' for 'all or most of the time'.

[2] See note at foot of Table 1, page 6.

organized *According to Age.* Also *Traditional Standard* pupils of the upper socio-economic group were more likely to be rated as disobedient than were *According to Age* children. Two traits on which *According to Age* pupils fared significantly worse than *Traditional Standard* pupils were 'withdrawn', where slightly more 'lower' class *According to Age* pupils were rated as this ($P < 0.5$), and 'unpleasurability', where fewer 'lower' class *According to Age* pupils were considered an unmixed pleasure to have in the class ($P < 0.1$). There were no differences between the two types of school organization on the rating—proneness to being teased (see Table 8).

TABLE 8: *A Comparison between Children in 'Traditional Standard' and 'According to Age' Schools of Teachers' Ratings on Maladjustment Traits*

CHILDREN RATED AS AT LEAST SOMETIMES:	UPPER SOCIO-ECONOMIC GROUP				LOWER SOCIO-ECONOMIC GROUP			
	TS	*AA*	x^2 *test*	*Inference*	*TS*	*AA*	x^2 *test*	*Inference*
Involved in fights	24%	18%	7·69	Significant at 1% level	33%	26%	7·34	Significant at 1% level
Withdrawn	14%	17%	1·75	Not Significant	17%	21%	4·98	Significant at 5% level
Disobedient	28%	21%	9·69	Significant at 1% level	31%	31%	0·02	Not Significant
Unpleasurable	14%	14%	0·00	Not Significant	21%	30%	15·15	Significant at 0·1% level
Teased	14%	13%	1·12	Not Significant	17%	18%	0·15	Not Significant
Number of pupils	749	626			674	644		

In terms of their combined 'total maladjustment rating' no significant difference emerged between the two types of school organization. These figures, however, are for the total number of children in the schools, no distinction being made for those children most affected by the prevailing philosophy of the school, i.e. children placed away from their own year-group by reason of being 'older' or 'younger' in *According to Age* schools, or being 'promoted' or 'demoted' in *Traditional Standard* schools. ('Total maladjustment rating' based on individual trait scores combined.)

5.2 Comparative 'Cohesion' of Classes

A specially prepared sociomatrix was administered to each class taking part in the Small Schools study. Teachers were asked to mark the first and second choice of friends made by each child in their class.

They were also asked to mark in those children who did not feel that they had a best friend and/or second best friend in their own class but who wished to choose a friend from another class in the same school.

An identification was made of the 'mutual' pairs of friends in each class (i.e. those pairs of children who had chosen each other as best or second-best friends). Using this information, a 'class cohesion' index (Co.) was established for each class. This was defined as:

$$\frac{\text{The number of mutual pairs}}{\text{The possible number of mutual pairs}}$$

With the number of choices restricted to two, the possible number of mutual pairs can be shown to equal the number of pupils in the class. The index thus provides a measure of the 'solidarity' and 'climate of friendliness' of the classes under review.

The results indicated that, in general, classes in *According to Age* schools tended to have a higher degree of cohesion than classes in *Traditional Standard* schools. This result presumably reflects the greater number of classes with a comparatively wide age-spread to be found in *Traditional Standard* schools. As will be discussed in Section 8, there was a significant tendency for the class cohesion to drop as the age-spread widened. This was evident in both types of school, although the level was consistently slightly higher in *According to Age* than in comparable *Traditional Standard* classes (see Section 8).

5.3 Conclusions

1. In terms of overall maladjustment ratings, no significant difference emerged between the two types of school, although on individual traits differences did emerge.

2. For both socio-economic groups, fighting was more associated with *Traditional Standard* pupils. Of the other traits, disobedience was more prevalent for the upper socio-economic group in *Traditional Standard* schools, and 'withdrawn' and 'unpleasurable' were more associated with *According to Age* schools for the lower (classes 4 and 5) socio-economic group.

3. Classes in *Traditional Standard* schools tended to be less 'cohesive', in terms of the mutual friendships within the class, than were classes in *According to Age* schools.

PART II

The Mixed-Age Class

COMPARISONS have so far been made between *Traditional Standard* and *According to Age* schools in terms of pupils' attainments and scores on various measures of social adjustment, and teachers' practices and characteristics in the two types of school. These figures relate to the total number of children in these schools, whereas the children who will be most affected by the particular type of organization will be those who, by reason of age or perceived ability, have been separated from their own year-group.

Sections 6, 7 and 8 present a study of the mixed-age class. It will be recalled that the schools in the Small Schools study were all of less than eight classes. Schools of this size were considered in the April 1965 report ('Junior schools and their type of school organization') under two headings, (a) 'Middle-sized' schools having five, six or seven junior classes, and (b) 'Small' schools having four or less junior classes.

In the 'Middle-sized' school, where the head is obliged to divide his four year-groups into five, six or seven classes, he is forced by circumstances to form classes of mixed year-groups. The four-class 'Small' junior school has one class for each year-group, providing the numbers in each group are equal. When this is not the case, the head must, of course, form mixed-age classes to equalize numbers at least to some extent. Small schools which have fewer classes than year-groups can only accommodate their pupils by forming classes of more than one year-group.

In the Survey of 'Junior schools and their type of organization', it was found that approximately 72 per cent of the children attending small schools (i.e. 31 per cent of all junior children) were in classes composed of two or more year-groups. Forty-three per cent of the pupils in middle-sized schools were in mixed-age classes (25 per cent of all juniors attend middle-sized schools).

It seemed that having more than one year-group in a class could well have important consequences for individual pupils, perhaps as important as those of the organization of the school as a whole. It was, therefore, decided to complement the study of *Traditional Standard* and *According to Age* schools by a consideration of 'mixed-age' classes. How do teachers deal with these classes in terms of grouping and teaching method? How do they perceive the ability of pupils of widely varying ages? What factors affect promotion or demotion and how do these pupils emerge on measures of maladjustment? All these aspects are examined in the following sections. (For definition of year-group, see para. 3.1.)

The Prevalence of the Mixed-Age Class

6.1 Percentage of Pupils in 'Traditional Standard' and 'According to Age' Schools in Classes of Pure/Mixed Year-Groups

It should first be noted that, of the 28 schools included in the sample of smaller schools, only two *Traditional Standard* schools had five classes. All *According to Age* schools, and the remaining 12 *Traditional Standard* schools were of four or less classes.

TABLE 9: *Percentage of Pupils in Classes of Pure and Mixed-Year Groups in 'Traditional Standard' and 'According to Age' Schools*

CLASS COMPOSITION	TRADITIONAL STANDARD		ACCORDING TO AGE		TOTAL	
	Pure Year Groups N %	Mixed-Year Groups N %	Pure Year Groups N %	Mixed-Year Groups N %	Pure Year Groups N %	Mixed-Year Groups N %
1st year pupils	44	332	134	232	178	564
2nd year pupils	—	352	136	208	136	560
3rd year pupils	—	348	123	214	123	562
4th year pupils	39	321	162	177	201	498
Total	83 6%	1,353 94%	555 40%	831 60%	638 23%	2,184 77%

As will be seen from Table 9, 77 per cent of the children in the sample were in classes of a mixed-year group. This proportion rose to 94 per cent of the children in *Traditional Standard* schools, and dropped to 60 per cent in *According to Age* schools. In particular, it should be noted that no second- or third-year pupils in *Traditional Standard* schools were in classes consisting of solely their own year-group.

6.2 The Composition of Mixed-Age Classes

An analysis of the composition of classes indicated that the most prevalent mixed-age classes were those combining third- and fourth-year pupils, with—in *Traditional Standard* schools—some second-year pupils too (see Table 10).

TABLE 10: *The Composition of Mixed-Age Classes*

	2 YEAR-GROUPS				3 YEAR-GROUPS			4 YEAR-GROUPS		5 YEAR-GROUPS	TOTAL NUMBER OF PUPILS
	Inf/ 1st year	*1st/ 2nd year*	*2nd/ 3rd year*	*3rd/ 4th year*	*Inf/ 1st/ 2nd year*	*1st/ 2nd/ 3rd year*	*2nd/ 3rd/ 4th year*	*Inf/ 1st/ 2nd/ 3rd year*	*1st/ 2nd/ 3rd/ 4th year*	*Inf/ 1st/ 2nd/ 3rd/ 4th year*	
TS	1%	16%	8%	22%	11%	11%	21%	4%	4%	1%	1,351 (100%)
AA	6%	17%	20%	31%	3%	16%	3%	—	4%	—	831 (100%)

In *According to Age* schools the majority of mixed-age classes (74 per cent) consist of a combination of two year-groups only; in *Traditional Standard* schools, however, 52 per cent consist of classes combining three year-groups or more.

6.3 The Age-Spread of Pure/Mixed-Age Classes

Clearly the possibility of achieving classes consisting of pupils all in one year-group is limited in the smaller school; it is non-existent where two- or three-class schools are concerned.

In order to ascertain the age-range within the class, a more reasonable index than administrative 'year-groups', is the age-spread of the pupils. For example, a class in which the pupils' ages at the beginning of the school year range from 7 yrs. 10 ms. to 8 yrs. 9 ms. is as homogeneous in terms of age as one consisting of one 'year-group', even though administratively it is a 'mixed-age' class.

In order to study the age-spread of the class, the standard deviation[1] of age in months was calculated for each class, with the following results:

[1] The Standard Deviation is a measure of dispersion. The smaller the SD the more homogeneous the group under consideration, since approximately two-thirds of the sample will fall within 1 SD above or below the mean. Thus, in the case of children's ages, a SD of 3 months indicates that 66 per cent of the class were aged within three months of the average for that class. A SD of 12 months would indicate that 66 per cent of the class were up to 12 months older or younger than the average age of the class.

TABLE 11: *The Age-Spread of Classes consisting of Pure/Mixed-Year Groups*

SD OF AGE IN MONTHS	COMPOSITION OF THE CLASS											
	Traditional Standard						According to Age					
	Pure Year gp.	Two year gp.	Three year gp.	Four year gp.	Five year gp.	Total	Pure Year gp.	Two year gp.	Three year gp.	Four year gp.	Five year gp.	Total
3.0– 4.0	3	2				5	17	5				22
4.1– 5.0		2	1			3		3	1			4
5.1– 6.0		7	1			8		6	1			7
6.1– 7.0		3	2			5		1	1			2
7.1– 8.0		1	6			7		2	1			3
8.1– 9.0			3			3						
9.1–10.0			3			3			1	1		2
10.1–11.0												
11.1–12.0				1		1						
12.1–13.0				1		1						
Total	3	15	16	2	0	36	17	17	5	1	0	40
Classes where full age-range not known		4	4	2	1	11		6	1			7

The Standard Deviation is, of course, a measure of general distribution, and as such not sensitive to any great extent to the presence of one or two class members who might fall well above or below the age of the majority of their classmates.

As will be seen from Table 11, in over half the *According to Age* classes, where the age-span was known, the age of the majority of pupils fell within an eight months span, and 33 of the 40 classes had a SD of six months or less; only 7 *According to Age* classes had a SD of over six months. Conversely, of the 36 *Traditional Standard* classes for which full data were available, 20 had a SD of over six months.

6.4 **The Relationship between Size of School and the Age-Span of Classes**

Clearly, the possibility of achieving classes of a relatively narrow age-span is limited in smaller schools by the number of classes in the school. Whatever the philosophy guiding pupils' allocation to a class, a two-class school can scarcely hope to achieve classes of as narrow an age-range (or ability range) as is possible in a four- or five-class school.

A comparison between the two types of school organization, in terms of the number of classes in the school, revealed that few *Traditional Standard* schools had as narrow an age-span as had comparable (in terms of size of school) *According to Age* schools. It is interesting to note that even in *According to Age* schools some two-class schools achieve classes of a narrower age-range than do some three-class schools; and some of these, in turn, have a narrower age-range than is shown by some four-class schools (see Table 12). The age-spread of classes in the *According to Age* schools will, of course, also depend upon the number of children of each age.

TABLE 12: *Relationship between the Size of School and the Age-Span of Classes*

SD OF AGE IN MONTHS	TRADITIONAL STANDARD					ACCORDING TO AGE				TOTAL
	2 class schools	3 class schools	4 class schools	5 class schools	Total	2 class schools	3 class schools	4 class schools	5 class schools	
3.1– 4.0			2	3	5			22		22
4.1– 5.0			2	1	3		1	3		4
5.1– 6.0		3	3	2	8	2	2	3		7
6.1– 7.0	1		3	1	5	2				2
7.1– 8.0		3	2	2	7		3			3
8.1– 9.0	1		2		3					
9.1–10.0	3				3	2				2
10.1–11.0										
11.1–12.0		1			1					
12.1–13.0	1				1					
Total	6	7	14	9	36	6	6	28	0	40
Classes where full age-range not known	2	2	6	1	11		3	4		7

6.5 Conclusions

1. In both types of school the majority of pupils found themselves in classes of mixed year-groups; in *Traditional Standard* schools 94 per cent, in *According to Age* schools 60 per cent.

2. In both types of school the most common mixed-age class consisted of third- and fourth-year pupils. Also prevalent in *Traditional Standard* schools were classes uniting second-, third- and fourth-year pupils.

3. In terms of the age-span within the classes, the majority of *According to Age* schools achieved a narrower spread of ages than did the *Traditional Standard* schools.

4. Whilst, in both types of school organization, the age-span of classes tended to narrow as the number of classes in the school increased, there was a considerable degree of 'overlap'. This was particularly interesting in the case of *According to Age* schools, where one would expect the declared policy of the school to apportion children to classes solely on the basis of age, to result in a consistent narrowing of the age-span as the number of classes increased.

32

SECTION SEVEN

The Teachers and the Mixed-Age Class

7.1 Introduction

Mention has already been made (Section 2) of the fact that no significant overall differences emerged between the *Traditional Standard* and *According to Age* schools in terms of the age and experience of their teachers, the incidence of 'progressive' or 'traditional' type lessons, grouping practices and seating arrangements.

In view of the prevalence, in both types of smaller school, of classes composed of pupils from two or more year-groups, it was felt advisable to complement the comparisons between the types of school organization, by a study of teachers' classes, with a relatively narrow and wide age-span.

For the purposes of these comparisons the standard deviation of the spread of ages of children in the class was taken, rather than the number of administrative 'year-groups' represented on the class register.

Comparisons were made in terms of

    (a) Grouping practices and individual teaching for Reading, English and Arithmetic;

    (b) Seating arrangements in the class;

    (c) The incidence of 'traditional' and 'progressive' type lessons;

    (d) The relationship between teachers' ability ratings and their pupils' performance on the Primary Verbal test.

33

7.2 Grouping Practices and Individual Teaching

Teachers were asked how their classes were grouped for lessons in Arithmetic, Reading and English. Responses were classified under the following headings:

(a) Taught as a class;

(b) In groups of mixed ability;

(c) In groups of similar ability;

(d) Individually.

1. *Arithmetic Grouping.* Teaching the class as a whole, or in groups of mixed ability, was only employed in classes of a comparatively narrow age-spread (SD of six months or less). As the age-spread widened there was an increased tendency to employ similar ability-grouping, and (especially for the widest age-span) individual teaching (see Table 13).

TABLE 13: *Comparison of Arithmetic Grouping in Classes of Differing Age-Spans*

SD OF AGE IN MONTHS	TAUGHT AS A CLASS	IN GROUPS OF MIXED ABILITY	IN GROUPS OF SIMILAR ABILITY	INDIVI-DUALLY	BY A COM-BINATION OF 2 OR MORE METHODS	TOTAL	REJECTS
3.0– 6.0	3	3	21	10	11	48	1
6.1– 9.0	0	0	12	5	3	20	
9.1–13.0	0	0	1	3	3	7	
Total	3	3	34	18	17	75	1
Classes where full age-range not known	1	0	9	5	3	18	

2. *Reading Grouping.* Reading was taught to the class as a whole in only one class, and was no longer taught as a separate subject in a sizeable number of classes, which accounts for the number of 'rejects' among the responses.

As with Arithmetic grouping, class teaching and groups of mixed ability were only employed by a minority of teachers of classes of narrow age-range. Similar ability grouping accounted for approximately a third of narrow age-range classes and just a half of other classes. Individual teaching was also more popular amongst teachers of classes more varied in age-range, accounting for roughly 40 per cent of these classes, as against just under a quarter of narrow age-range classes (see Table 14).

TABLE 14: *Comparison of Reading Grouping in Classes of Differing Age-Spans*

SD OF AGE IN MONTHS	TAUGHT AS A CLASS	IN GROUPS OF MIXED ABILITY	IN GROUPS OF SIMILAR ABILITY	INDIVI-DUALLY	BY A COM-BINATION OF 2 OR MORE METHODS	TOTAL	REJECTS
3.0– 6.0	1	5	14	10	13	43	6
6.1– 9.0	0	0	8	6	1	15	5
9.1–13.0	0	0	2	2	2	6	1
Total	1	5	24	18	16	64	12
Classes where full age-range not known	1		5	8	3	17	1

3. *English Grouping.* Class teaching was much more popular for English than for other subjects, and was not restricted to classes of a narrow age-range. In all, 18 of the 48 classes of standard deviation 3.0–6.0 months were taught exclusively as a class for English, as were seven of the 27 classes with a wider age-spread (see Table 15).

TABLE 15: *Comparison of English Grouping in Classes of Differing Age-Spans*

SD OF AGE IN MONTHS	TAUGHT AS A CLASS	IN GROUPS OF MIXED ABILITY	IN GROUPS OF SIMILAR ABILITY	INDIVI-DUALLY	BY A COM-BINATION OF 2 OR MORE METHODS	TOTAL	REJECTS
3.0– 6.0	18	5	9	4	12	48	1
6.1– 9.0	5	0	6	2	7	20	
9.1–13.0	2	0	1	2	2	7	
Total	25	5	16	8	21	75	1
Classes where full age-range not known	4	1	6	1	6	18	

Grouping Practices Employed with Classes of Differing Age-Spans in 'Traditional Standard' v. 'According to Age' Schools

Comparisons made between teachers in *Traditional Standard* and *According to Age* schools in their methods of teaching classes of narrower or wider age-spread revealed no significant differences, although there was a tendency, in all three subjects, for *According to Age* class teachers to make more use of similar ability grouping with classes of a narrow age-range than did their *Traditional Standard* counterparts.

35

Where they were handling classes of a relatively wide age-range, teachers from both types of school adopted similar strategies, generally avoiding class teaching (apart from English) and groups of mixed ability, and concentrating on groups of similar ability within the class.

7.3 Seating Arrangement in the Class

Class teachers were also asked about the seating arrangements in their classes, and asked whether these arrangements were in force for all or part of the time.

On the basis of their replies, classes were categorized as follows:

(a) *Streamed within the class for most of the time*, i.e. for at least three subjects—or for two subjects and, in addition, for part of the time on 'general ability'. A free choice of seats was either never permitted or only allowed for a limited part of the time, e.g. in Art or Craft lessons.

(b) *Streamed within the class for part of the time*, i.e. pupils were streamed for part of the time for one or two subjects.

(c) *Not streamed within the class*, i.e. pupils were either allowed a free choice of seat or given seats on some basis other than ability or attainment, such as

(i) year-group, or

(ii) 'size of desks, chairs and children'.

The distribution of seating arrangements in terms of the age-spread of classes was as follows:

TABLE 16: *Seating Arrangements in Classes of Differing Age-Spans*

SD OF AGE IN MONTHS	STREAMED FOR ALL OR MOST OF THE TIME	STREAMED SOME OF THE TIME	COMPLETE FREE CHOICE	TOTAL
3.0– 6.0	14	26	9	49
6.1– 9.0	10	7	3	20
9.1–13.0	1	2	4	7
Total	25	35	16	76

Clearly no trends are discernible from these figures. Whatever the constitution of the class, streaming for at least part of the time is widely favoured, except in the case of classes with a wide age-span (SD 9.1–13.0 months). Presumably the higher incidence of free choice of seats for these classes reflects the wider use made here of individual teaching.

In terms of comparisons between seating arrangements for mixed-age classes in the two types of school, little difference was evident. Any attempts at comparisons are, in any case, made difficult by the very small number of *According to Age* classes (seven classes) which fall into either of the two categories of wider age-span.

7.4 'Traditional' and 'Progressive' Teaching Methods

There were no significant differences between classes of differing age-ranges in terms of their teachers' scores on the scales of 'traditional' and 'progressive' type lessons.[1]

In the study of larger junior schools, 'streamed' and 'non-streamed' schools were found to have significantly different mean scores on both these scales, the streamed schools being more 'traditional' and the non-streamed schools more 'progressive'. The incidence of 'traditional' and 'progressive' type lessons varied widely in the small schools sample, but no significant differences could be established. Results for the smaller schools generally fell between those of larger streamed and non-streamed schools.

7.5 A Comparison of the Teachers' Ability Ratings with their Pupils' Performance on the Primary Verbal Test

Class teachers were asked to rate the 'general ability' of each pupil in the class, *in relation to his age-group*. The original rating was on a five-point scale, but for the purposes of our analysis the ratings were regrouped as:

(a) Above average—denoting the certainty or possibility of a Grammar school place or equivalent ability level.

(b) Average.

(c) Below average—possibly or definitely backward.

A sample was drawn of all the second-year children taking part in the study. This was subdivided as follows:

(a) Mixed-age classes where the second-year children were the *youngest* in the class i.e. classes composed of 2nd/3rd or 2nd/3rd/4th year children.

(b) Mixed-age classes where the second-year children came in the *middle* of the class i.e. classes composed of 1st/2nd/3rd year children or of children of all four year-groups.

(c) Classes where the second-year children were the *oldest* in the class i.e. classes of Infants/1st/2nd or of 1st/2nd year children.

A comparison was made of the degree to which 'oldest' and 'youngest' second-year children had apparently been over- or under-rated by their teachers. It was considered that an 'above average'

[1] For details see: BARKER LUNN, J. C. (1967). 'The effects of streaming and non-streaming in junior schools: Second interim report', *New Research in Education*, vol. 1, pp. 46-75. (Distributed by NFER).

child should have a Primary Verbal raw score of more than one standard deviation above the mean score for all second-year children; that an 'average' child's score should fall within one standard deviation above or below the mean, and that a score of more than one standard deviation below the mean should be obtained by children rated 'below' average. It should be borne in mind that the teachers had not been asked to rate to these specific criteria, and that a certain amount of error must be ascribed to this.

The following table shows the results of this comparison.

TABLE 17: *A Comparison of the Degree to which Children of Similar Age, but either 'Youngest' or 'Oldest' in their Class, are either Over- or Under-Rated by their Teachers*

	2ND YEAR CHILDREN 'OLDEST' IN THE CLASS	2ND YEAR CHILDREN 'YOUNGEST' IN THE CLASS
Children rated 'above average' % *over-rated* i.e. children who did not score more than 1 SD above the mean	N = 24 62%	N = 62 26%
Children rated as 'average' % *over-rated* i.e. children scoring more than 1 SD below the mean % *under-rated* i.e. children scoring more than 1 SD above the mean	N = 93 17% 3%	N = 72 7% 21%
Children rated 'below average' % *under-rated* i.e. children scoring within 1 SD of the mean	N = 48 37%	N = 29 59%

Even allowing for error arising from the different criteria used, there is a marked tendency for these children, when they are the 'oldest' in the class, to be over-rated for ability and a corresponding tendency for 'youngest' children, handicapped by relative immaturity, to be under-rated in comparison with their classmates. (This tendency for error reached statistical significance.)

In view of this finding, a comparison was made of the teachers' accuracy in rating classes composed purely of second-year children, and that displayed in the rating of mixed-age classes. Correlations did not in fact vary. Teachers displayed the same degree of accuracy, and the same proportion of errors, in all cases where they rated ability, but only in the case of 'youngest' or 'oldest' children in the class were tendencies consistently to under- or over-rate observable.

7.6 Conclusions

1. Groups of mixed ability for teaching the '3R's' were only found in classes of a relatively narrow age-range. As the age-range of the class widened, there was an increasing tendency for similar ability grouping or individual teaching for the '3R's' to be adopted. This tendency was evident in both *According to Age* and *Traditional Standard* schools, indicating that *Traditional Standard* teachers also perceived a wider 'spread' of interests, attainments and maturity in the mixed-age class, even when class grouping had been made in an attempt to produce homogeneity.

2. In all types of class, streaming for subject teaching was favoured for at least some of the time.

3. There was no evidence to suggest that the incidence of 'traditional' or 'progressive' type lessons differs between classes of differing age-spreads.

4. It would seem clear that, in the context of a mixed-age class, teachers tend to over-rate the ability of the maturer 'older' children, and to under-rate the ability of the 'younger' children.

D

SECTION EIGHT

The Pupil in the Mixed-Age Class

8.1 Introduction

Whatever the educational philosophy behind the school organization, only a minority of pupils find themselves placed away from the mass of their own year-group.

What of those children who were placed away from their year-group in mixed-age classes, either by reason of their being 'younger' or 'older' than the majority of their year-group, as in *According to Age* schools, or in schools with *Traditional Standard* organization, by reason of their perceived ability?

To what extent do pupils' demotions or promotions in *Traditional Standard* schools accord with teachers' ratings of ability, and children's performance as measured by test results? What other factors influence a child's possibilities of promotion or demotion?

For children in a minority away from their year-group, is either form of school organization associated with traits of maladjustment or social isolation?

This section presents the data obtained on the 'minority' groups in mixed-age classes in *Traditional Standard* and *According to Age* schools. For the purpose of these comparisons, the following definitions of pupil status were employed:

(1) *According to Age 'older' children:* the older children of a year-group have been put up with an older year-group.

(2) *According to Age 'younger' children:* the younger children of a year-group have been kept down with a younger year-group.

(3) *Traditional Standard 'promoted' children:* 'brighter' children in a class with children a year older.

(4) *Traditional Standard 'demoted' children:* 'duller' children in a class with children a year younger.

These wide definitions of pupil status in *Traditional Standard* schools tended to obscure the difference between 'pure' promotion, which was achieved at the expense of other older pupils, or the 'pure' demotion involved in being in a class lower than that of other younger children, and the mere 'moving up' or being 'kept down' which the organization of smaller schools with fewer classes tends to necessitate. The reality is that the groups of 'promoted' children contain two fairly distinct sub-groups:

    (a) children promoted at the expense of other older children, i.e. a 'crossover'; less than 25 per cent of the 'brightest' of a year-group with children one year older;

    (b) *more* than 25 per cent of the 'brightest' of a year-group in a class with children a year older (no 'crossover').

Similarly, the wide definition of 'demotion' included two sub-groups:

    (a) children demoted to make room for 'brighter' younger children, i.e. a 'crossover'; less than 25 per cent of the 'dullest' of a year-group with children one year younger;

    (b) more than 25 per cent of the 'dullest' of a year-group in a class with children a year younger (no 'crossover').

With a view to clarifying the position of those children who were truly 'promoted' or 'demoted' in accordance with the *Traditional Standard* philosophy of school organization, rather than as a result of the mere exigencies of distributing pupils to the limited number of classes available in a small school, analyses were also carried out employing narrower definitions of 'promotion' or 'demotion'. These sub-groups are referred to as 'pure promotion' and 'pure demotion'.

    (5) *Traditional Standard 'pure promotion':* includes only those children promoted at the expense of other older children, and where less than 25 per cent of the 'brightest' of a year-group are with children a year older.

    (6) *Traditional Standard 'pure demotion':* includes only those children demoted to make way for 'brighter', younger children, and where less than 25 per cent of the 'dullest' of a year-group are with children a year younger.

8.2 **Pupil Status and its Relation to Teachers' Ability Ratings**

Class teachers were asked to rate their pupils on the following five-point scale:

    1. 'Certain of a Grammar school place or equivalent ability level'.

    2. 'Above average, possible Grammar school place'.

    3. 'Average'.

    4. 'Below average and possibly backward'.

    5. 'Dull and definitely backward'.

In the interests of conciseness, these five ratings were combined into three categories, i.e. 'Above average', 'Average' and 'Below average'. The results of the comparisons are set out in the following tables.

TABLE 18: *Comparative Ability Ratings among Children in 'According to Age' Schools*

	'ACCORDING TO AGE' SCHOOLS					
	'Older' children 'put up'		Children with own year-group		'Younger' children 'kept down'	
	N	%	N	%	N	%
Above average ability	16	26	351	28	22	31
Average ability	32	53	546	44	26	36
Below average ability	13	21	356	28	24	33
Total	61	100	1,253	100	72	100

These differences between ratings of 'older' children 'put up' with an older year-group, 'younger' children 'kept down', and children in a class composed mainly of their own year-group do not reach statistical significance, i.e. in *According to Age* schools, ratings of ability do not appear to bear a relationship to pupils' class status.

TABLE 19: *Comparative Ability Ratings among Children in 'Traditional Standard' Schools*

	'TRADITIONAL STANDARD' SCHOOLS							
	All demoted children		Children with own year-group		All promoted children		Others	
	N	%	N	%	N	%	N	%
Above average ability	23	9	195	22	109	44	7	11
Average ability	120	48	450	52	118	47	18	28
Below average ability	107	43	227	26	22	9	40	61
Total	250	100	872	100	249	100	65	100

The declared policy of the schools has led one to expect that the majority of 'promoted' children would be rated as of 'above average ability', and that the majority of 'demoted' children would be rated as 'below average'.

In neither instance was this the case. The majority of these children were rated 'average' and the small number of 'promoted' children rated 'below average' (9 per cent) and 'demoted' children rated 'above average' (9 per cent) raised the question as to why these children had ever been moved at all. The 'promoted' children would be the 'youngest' in their classes and on the basis of our results, it is expected that they would tend to be under-rated (see page 37) and that there would be a corresponding tendency to over-rate the 'demoted' children. But it is doubted whether this tendency alone would suffice to explain the minority of children whose allocation appeared positively mistaken.

An investigation of the children's standardized scores on the Primary Verbal test showed that the majority were of average ability i.e. they scored 86–115. The following table shows the distribution.

TABLE 20: *Standardized Primary Verbal Scores of 'Inexplicably Allocated' Children*

STANDARDIZED PRIMARY VERBAL score	'PROMOTED' CHILDREN RATED BELOW AVERAGE	'DEMOTED' CHILDREN RATED ABOVE AVERAGE
Over 115	0	2
100–115	7	8
86–100	2	3
85 and under	7	1
Absent and rejects†	6	9
Total	22	23

† The Primary Verbal test was not administered to the first-year juniors.

Social class as rated by the teacher did not seem to have influenced this allocation, as the 'promoted' children rated 'below average' tended to be of a lower social class than the 'demoted' group under review. The teachers' judgements on ability appeared to relate above all to the children's attitude to school work, as is shown by the following distribution of teachers' assessments.

TABLE 21: *Attitude to School Work of 'Inexplicably Allocated' Children*

ATTITUDE TO SCHOOL WORK (TEACHERS' ASSESSMENT)	'PROMOTED' CHILDREN RATED BELOW AVERAGE	'DEMOTED' CHILDREN RATED ABOVE AVERAGE
A poor worker	13	1
An average worker	8	3
A hard worker	1	12
A very hard worker	0	7
Total	22	23

Clearly the 22 'promoted' children, rated by their teachers as of below average ability, were not 'put up' by reason of their somewhat dilatory attitude to school work, nor were the 23 'demoted' children of perceived above-average ability 'put down' as a reward for their diligence.

Rather these children's attitudes to school work would seem to be a result of their allocation to a class where a different year-group predominates. One can hypothesize that the 'promoted' group of children of mainly average ability may have become discouraged by competition with an older class, and the 'demoted' average children, finding their relative maturity a help to them, may have been encouraged to elevate themselves to their work. The numbers are small, but the tendency is there.

8.3 Teachers' Ability Ratings of the 'Pure Promoted' and 'Pure Demoted' Children in 'Traditional Standard' Schools

When one takes the figures for those groups of children who had been definitely 'put up' or 'kept down' as a function of the educational philosophy of the *Traditional Standard* school, rather than moved away from their year-group for administrative reasons, the picture of the 'promoted' and 'demoted' child becomes clearer.

In terms of teachers' ability ratings, only four children were 'inexplicably allocated' to a class: two, rated as 'above average ability', had been 'demoted', and two, rated as 'below average', had been 'promoted' (see Table 22).

TABLE 22: *Teachers' Comparative Ability Ratings of 'Pure Promoted' and 'Pure Demoted' Children*

	ABOVE AVERAGE ABILITY		AVERAGE ABILITY		BELOW AVERAGE ABILITY		TOTAL	
	N	%	N	%	N	%	N	%
'Pure Demoted'	2	4	19	28	44	68	65	100
'Pure Promoted'	48	55	38	43	2	2	88	100

All of these four 'inexplicably allocated' children in fact had average scores on the Primary Verbal test, but the two 'promoted' children rated as 'below average' were considered by their teachers to be 'poor workers', and the two 'demoted' children rated as 'above average' in ability were considered 'hard workers' or 'very hard workers'.

8.4 Pupil Status in Relation to Scores on Standardized Tests

As a further check upon the relationship between pupil class status and their levels of attainment, the scores obtained by 8-plus and 9-plus children on three attainment tests (Reading, English and Problem Arithmetic) were analysed in terms of the children's status in the class (i.e. 'younger', 'older' in *According to Age* schools, 'promoted' or 'demoted' in *Traditional Standard* schools; and 'with their own year-group', in both schools combined). Pupils were divided into three groups in terms of their performance on each test, i.e.

(a) 'High Scorers': who obtained scores more than 1 SD above the mean for their year-group.

(b) 'Medium Scorers': whose scores fell within 1 SD above or below the mean for their year-group.

(c) 'Low Scorers': whose scores were more than 1 SD below the mean for their year-group.

The distribution of scores is shown in the table below.

It will be seen that the great majority of both 'high' and 'low' scorers are, in fact, in classes where their own year-group predominates.

TABLE 23: *Distribution of Test Scores for 8-Plus and 9-Plus Children, in Terms of Pupils' Class Status*

CLASS STATUS		CHILDREN WITH OWN YEAR-GROUP		'DEMOTED' CHILDREN		'PROMOTED' CHILDREN		'YOUNGER' CHILDREN 'KEPT DOWN'		'OLDER' CHILDREN 'PUT UP'	
		N	%	N	%	N	%	N	%	N	%
READING 8+	Low Scores	64	16	22	18	5	5	4	11	1	5
	Med. Scores	282	72	94	78	75	68	30	81	16	76
	High Scores	45	12	5	4	30	27	3	8	4	19
	Total	391	100	121	100	110	100	37	100	21	100
ENGLISH 8+	Low Scores	67	17	26	21	3	3	4	11	1	5
	Med. Scores	267	68	89	74	83	75	28	76	15	71
	High Scores	57	15	6	5	24	22	5	13	5	24
	Total	391	100	121	100	110	100	37	100	21	100
PROBLEM 8+	Low Scores	56	14	25	21	4	4	0	0	1	5
	Med. Scores	287	74	91	75	80	73	28	76	16	76
	High Scores	48	12	5	4	26	23	9	24	4	19
	Total	391	100	121	100	110	100	37	100	21	100
READING 9+	Low Scores	71	14	17	30	1	2	5	28	0	0
	Med. Scores	377	76	37	66	33	54	11	61	8	89
	High Scores	52	10	2	4	27	44	2	11	1	11
	Total	500	100	56	100	61	100	18	100	9	100
ENGLISH 9+	Low Scores	75	15	17	30	0	0	4	22	1	11
	Med. Scores	414	83	39	70	56	92	13	72	8	89
	High Scores	11	2	0	0	5	8	1	6	0	0
	Total	500	100	56	100	61	100	18	100	9	100
PROBLEM 9+	Low Scores	82	16	18	32	3	5	4	22	0	0
	Med. Scores	344	69	38	68	31	51	14	78	7	78
	High Scores	74	15	0	0	27	44	0	0	2	22
	Total	500	100	56	100	61	100	18	100	9	100

Low Score = below 1 SD from the mean; Medium Score = within 1 SD from the mean; High Score = above 1 SD from the mean.

There is a marked (and not surprising) tendency for 'low' scorers to have been 'demoted' in schools where this policy prevails, and for 'high' scorers to have been 'promoted'—but once again there is a slight but fairly consistent tendency for completely 'inexplicable allocations', in that 'low' scorers have been 'promoted' and 'high' scorers 'demoted', admittedly in very small numbers, but in flat contradiction to the school's declared policy.

Where the narrower definitions of 'pure promotion' and 'pure demotion' are employed, no 'demoted' children achieved high scores on any of the tests, and no 'promoted' children scored below average on any of the tests.

8.5 The Age of 'Promoted' and 'Demoted' Children

A distribution by age of 'promoted' and 'demoted' children (in months) did indicate one possible source of error. Each year-group was sub-divided into three sub-groups, each with an age-range of four months, which will be subsequently referred to as 'oldest', 'middle' and 'youngest'. The distribution of 'promoted' and 'demoted' children within these sub-groups is shown in the following tables.

TABLE 24: *Distribution by Age of 'Demoted' Children*

	1ST YEAR		2ND YEAR		3RD YEAR		4TH YEAR		TOTAL	
	N	%	N	%	N	%	N	%	N	%
'Oldest' (born Sept.–Dec.)	6	18	18	15	5	9	12	32	41	17
'Middle' (born Jan.–April)	8	23	43	35	22	38	7	19	80	32
'Youngest' (born May–August)	20	59	60	50	30	53	18	49	128	51
Total	34	100	121	100	57	100	37	100	249	100

TABLE 25: *Distribution by Age of 'Promoted' Children*

	1ST YEAR		2ND YEAR		3RD YEAR		4TH YEAR		TOTAL	
	N	%	N	%	N	%	N	%	N	%
'Oldest' (born Sept.–Dec.)	40	52	45	41	27	44	No promotion possible from 4th year		112	45
'Middle' (born Jan.–April)	23	30	42	38	17	28			82	33
'Youngest' (born May–August)	14	18	23	21	17	28			54	22
Total	77	100	110	100	61	100			248	100

It can be seen that there is a very marked and consistent tendency for 'demoted' children to be among the youngest of their year-group and for 'promoted' children to be among the oldest. Differences in the length of infant schooling, in physical maturity and in accuracy of teachers' ability ratings are probably all factors contributing to this situation. But it is clear that, should 'promotion' and 'demotion' be thought desirable, they ought to be conducted on the basis of standardized tests rather than on present criteria which appear at times distinctly haphazard.

8.6 Behaviour Ratings of Pupils in a Minority Away from their Own Year-Group

On teachers' ratings of behaviour, how do pupils in a minority away from their year-group compare with children in a class with their own year-group? Do children in *Traditional Standard* schools 'demoted' or 'promoted' in terms of their perceived ability differ, more than 'younger' and 'older' children in *According to Age* schools, from their companions kept with their own age-group?

For each of the two types of school organization, minority pupils' behaviour ratings were compared with those of children in a class with their own year-group. The data on which comparisons were made were teachers' ratings of pupils':

(a) Attitude to work,

(b) Involvement in fights,

(c) Withdrawal,

(d) Disobedience,

(e) Unpleasurability,

(f) Proneness to being teased,

and also of pupils' sociometric score (for details of how this score was devised, see para. 5.2).

In *According to Age* schools, no significant differences on behaviour ratings were found between 'younger' children 'kept down', or 'older' children 'put up', and children in a class with their own year-group.

In *Traditional Standard* schools, in contrast, there was a marked tendency for 'demoted' children to be rated as less diligent in their school work, more prone to fighting, more inclined to disobedience, and less pleasurable to have in the class. 'Promoted' children tended to be rated as harder workers, less prone to fighting, more obedient and more pleasurable to have in the class. These differences were more evident when the groups of 'pure demoted' and 'pure promoted' children were considered in isolation from the 'split year-group' form of 'demotion' and 'promotion' (see Table 26).

TABLE 26: *Comparison of 'Demoted' and 'Promoted' Minorities with Pure Year-Groups in 'Traditional Standard' Schools, for Behaviour Ratings*

VARIABLE 1	VARIABLE 2	SEX	SIGNIFICANCE LEVEL	COMMENTS
ATTITUDE TO WORK	All demoted	Boys	0·1%	Proportionately fewer demoted boys rated 'very hard' or 'hard workers', more rated 'poor workers' or 'lazy'. Tendency for 'pure demoted' boys to be rated 'poor workers' or 'lazy'. (Significant at 1% level).
	All promoted	Boys	1%	Proportionately more promoted boys rated 'very hard workers', fewer coded 'lazy'. Tendency for 'pure promoted' boys to be rated 'very hard workers'. (Significant at 0·1% level).
	All demoted	Girls	Non Significant	Where 'pure demoted' considered, fewer demoted girls rated 'very hard' or 'hard workers'. More rated 'poor workers' or 'lazy'. (Significant at 1% level).
	All promoted	Girls	Non Significant	Remained non-significant for 'pure promoted' girls.
INVOLVEMENT IN FIGHTS	All demoted	Boys	5%	Proportionately fewer demoted boys rated as 'seldom' or 'never involved in fights'. Tendency for 'pure demoted' boys to fight. (Significant at 0·1% level).
	All promoted	Boys	Non Significant	Where 'pure promoted' boys considered, proportionately more were rated as 'seldom or never' involved in fights. (Significant at 1% level).
	All demoted	Girls	Non Significant	Remained non-significant for 'pure demoted' girls.
	All promoted	Girls	Non Significant	Where 'pure promoted' girls considered, proportionately more were rated as 'seldom or never' involved in fights. (Significant at 5% level).
DISOBEDIENT	All demoted	Boys	Non Significant	Where 'pure demoted' boys considered, proportionately fewer were rated 'seldom or never' disobedient. (Significant at 5% level).
	All promoted	Boys	Non Significant	For 'pure promoted' boys, proportionately more were rated 'seldom or never' disobedient. (Significant at 1% level).
	All demoted	Girls	1%	Proportionately fewer demoted girls rated 'seldom or never' disobedient. Tendency for 'pure demoted' girls to be rated disobedient. (Significant at 0·1% level).
	All promoted	Girls	Non Significant	Remained non-significant for 'pure promoted' girls.

Continued

VARIABLE 1	VARIABLE 2	SEX	SIGNIFI-CANCE LEVEL	COMMENTS
UNPLEASUR-ABILITY	All demoted	Boys	1%	Proportionately fewer demoted boys rated 'pleasurable most of the time'. Tendency for 'pure demoted' boys to be unpleasurable. (Significant at 1% level).
	All promoted	Boys	0·1%	Proportionately more promoted boys rated as 'pleasurable most of the time'. Tendency for 'pure promoted' boys to be rated pleasurable. (Significant at 0·1% level).
	All demoted	Girls	Non Significant	For 'pure demoted' girls, proportionately more were rated as only 'sometimes' or 'seldom or never' a pleasure and fewer were rated as 'pleasurable most of the time'. (Significant at 5% level).
	All promoted	Girls	5%	Proportionately more promoted girls rated as pleasurable 'most of the time', fewer were rated pleasurable only 'sometimes' or 'seldom or never'.
TEASED	All demoted	Boys	5%	Proportionately fewer demoted boys rated as 'seldom or never' teased. Tendency for 'pure demoted' boys to be teased. (Significant at 0·1% level).
	All promoted	Boys	Non Significant	Remained non-significant for 'pure promoted' boys.
	All demoted	Girls	Non Significant	For 'pure demoted' girls, proportionately fewer rated as 'seldom or never' teased. (Significant at 5% level).
	All promoted	Girls	Non Significant	Remained non-significant for 'pure promoted' girls.
WITHDRAWN				No significant differences between minority groups and children in a class with their own year-group.
SOCIOMETRIC SCORE	All demoted	Boys	Non Significant	Remained non-significant for 'pure demoted' boys.
	All promoted	Boys	Non Significant	Remained non-significant for 'pure promoted' boys.
	All demoted	Girls	0·1%	Proportionately more were social isolates. Tendency for 'pure demoted' girls to be social isolates. (Significant at 1% level).
	All promoted	Girls	0·1%	Proportionately more social isolates. Tendency for 'pure promoted' girls to be social isolates. (Significant at 0·1% level).

These behaviour traits covered by the survey can be considered as falling into two distinct categories:

(a) ratings concerned with the pupil's attitude towards school work and behaviour in class, i.e. attitude to work, disobedience, pleasurability;

(b) aspects of his relationships with his fellow pupils, i.e. involvement in fights, withdrawal, proneness to being teased and sociometric score.

In terms of those aspects of behaviour which relate to the pupil in class, a picture emerges of the 'demoted' children (both boys and girls) as poor workers, inclined to disobedience and not altogether pleasurable to their teachers. 'Promoted' children, in contrast, are rated (both boys and girls) as a pleasure to have in class, and the boys were also significantly better workers than were children in a class with their own year-group.

Where aspects of children's relationships with their fellow pupils are concerned, 'demoted' children show a slight tendency to be more the victims of teasing, maybe as a concomitant of which 'demoted' boys are more prone to fighting. Both 'promoted' and 'demoted' girls tend to be social isolates; however, this is the only trait on which 'promoted' children show signs of maladjustment, and it is significant that this is a peer rating, not a teacher rating.

How can one account for these differences? If traits of maladjustment were resulting purely from the experience of finding oneself in a class away from one's own year-group, one would expect both 'promoted' and 'demoted' children to show signs of disturbance. One would, moreover, expect parallel tendencies to be evident in 'older' or 'younger' children in *According to Age* schools. No such tendencies emerged.

Three explanations suggest themselves:

(a) It should be borne in mind that these behaviour traits were measured by teachers' ratings. It may be that teachers in *Traditional Standard* schools, working in a climate of streaming by merit, are influenced in their ratings of pupils' behaviour by their knowledge that pupils have been 'promoted' or 'demoted' on their perceived ability. This may lead to a generally improved perception of 'promoted' pupils, on behavioural traits; conversely, 'demoted' children may tend to be generally down-graded in a teacher's estimation.

(b) It may be that in *Traditional Standard* schools, decisions to 'promote' or 'demote' children are partly influenced, especially in marginal cases of children of average ability, by pupils' general comportment, so that the differences discussed here are partly the cause of a pupil's class status, rather than resulting from it.

If either of these two explanations is the case, then one would not expect either form of school organization overall to be more associated with traits of maladjustment; if explanation (a) were correct, then the over-estimations of 'promoted' children given by *Traditional Standard* teachers would tend to cancel out under-estimations of 'demoted' children; if (b) were the case, one would anticipate that roughly the same proportion of children in both types of school would show signs of some maladjustment, but that these traits would not vary according to pupil status in *According to Age* schools.

A third explanation of the data would be that these traits of maladjustment evident in *Traditional Standard* 'demoted' children were real (not merely due to teachers' over- or under-estimations) and resulted from a pupil's status in the class, rather than being partly a reason for placement, i.e.

(c) Children themselves may be reacting to what they perceive as a 'promotion' with the fillip it may give to the morale, or a 'demotion' with its disturbing effects on the pupil's enthusiasm for his class work and confidence in his relationship with his fellow pupils.

If this is the case, then one would expect a greater incidence of traits of maladjustment in *Traditional Standard* than *According to Age* schools, since the method of school organization is itself contributing to the disturbance of its children.

The data for the overall incidence of traits of maladjustment in the two types of schools are not sufficiently clear-cut for us to conclude with any degree of confidence how much weight should be attributed to any of these three alternative explanations (see Section 5). Certainly a greater proportion of *Traditional Standard* pupils were considered prone to fighting, and *Traditional Standard* classes did tend to have a lower degree of cohesion; but against this, a greater proportion of *According to Age* children were rated as withdrawn and not altogether pleasurable.

Whatever the factors underlying these behaviour ratings of children in *Traditional Standard* schools, a clear picture does emerge of the 'demoted' child as being regarded by his (or her) teacher as being not merely distinct from his age mates in terms of his level of attainment, but also as inferior in terms of his application to his studies, his obedience and pleasurability and his having more problems in his relationship with his fellow pupils. 'Promoted' children, in their teachers' eyes, represent to some extent an *élite* in their comportment in class and, to a slight extent, in their relationships inside the class.

8.7 Conclusions

1. In *According to Age* schools, pupils' class status does not appear to bear any relationship to teachers' ability ratings.

2. In *Traditional Standard* schools, the majority of both 'demoted' and 'promoted' children were in fact rated as of 'average ability'.

3. Where teachers' ratings of ability appeared in contradiction with a pupil's actual class status, his perceived attitude to school work appeared an important contribution to this 'inexplicable' rating.

4. The majority of all groups of children, whether 'older' or 'younger' in *According to Age* schools, 'promoted' or 'demoted' in *Traditional Standard* schools, or with their own year-group, tended to achieve average scores on standardized tests. There were, however, consistently some pupils whose test scores would suggest they had been mistakenly allocated to their class.

5. An important source of error in the allocation of pupils to classes in *Traditional Standard* schools would appear to be their relative age within their year-group. Consistently the 'youngest' of a year-group tended to be 'demoted' and the 'oldest' to be 'promoted'.

6. In *According to Age* schools no significant differences were found, on teachers' ratings of various behaviour traits, between 'younger' children 'kept down' or 'older' children 'put up', and children in a class with their own year-group. In contrast, in *Traditional Standard* schools there was a consistent tendency for more 'demoted' children to manifest signs of disturbance and for 'promoted' children to be rated better than their companions in classes with their own year-group.

The data available are not conclusive enough to state with any degree of confidence whether this tendency is the result of teachers' over- and under-estimations or of the fact that some behaviour is partly adopted as a criterion of allocation to classes, or whether the 'demotion' or 'promotion' has had an effect on the children's behaviour.

SECTION NINE

Summary and Conclusions

A COMPARATIVE study was made of the effects of different types of school organization on pupils' achievements and behaviour. This study was carried out in Small Schools[1] in 1965 at the request of the Department of Education and Science.

The two main forms of organization found in small schools are the *Traditional Standard* and *According to Age* methods.

The *Traditional Standard* method involves allocation of children to classes roughly according to age but with some promotion of the more able pupils and retention, or keeping back, of the less able with a class of younger children. The effect of this is to produce a wide age-range, a wide ability range but a more or less homogeneous level of attainment within the class.

On the other hand, the *According to Age* method adheres strictly to the criterion of age (in months), and children are assigned to classes without reference to their attainment or ability.

A particular problem of the small school is that with the exception of the four-class school, there are more year-groups than classes, and the heads may be forced by these circumstances to split a year-group of pupils and/or to put more than one year-group in a class. In doing this, the criterion of allocation of pupils to classes may be either age or achievement, according to whether the school's accepted policy is *According to Age* or *Traditional Standard* method.

The NFER Survey of Types of Junior School Organization[2] discussed some of the problems which may arise in the small school.

---

[1] Small Schools are defined as having four junior classes or fewer.

[2] BARKER LUNN, J. C. (1967). 'The effects of streaming and other forms of grouping in junior schools: Interim report', *New Research in Education*, vol. 1, pp. 4-45. (Distributed by NFER).

Children in a year-group are regarded, for all administrative purposes, as being effectively the same age. For example, they take the '11-Plus' at the same time and they leave junior school at the same time. The Survey Report says:

> 'Children who are separated from the rest of their year-group may therefore suffer some disadvantage. "Younger" children kept back a year may miss the stimulus provided by companionship with members of their own year-group; some class lessons (e.g. stories) will probably be more appropriate to the other younger members of the class. Furthermore, keeping back slower children and promoting bright children may create problems of the kind that were outlined in the 1931 Report on the Primary School.'[1]

The NFER Survey of School Organizations revealed some of the problems and difficulties of the small school, and it was with these in mind that the research was set up.

The research had two main aims:

(1) to compare the two types of organization found in small schools and their effects on pupils' attainments and behaviour;

(2) to investigate the effects of promotion and demotion as found in small schools; also the effect of keeping back 'younger' pupils and putting up 'older' pupils which is the policy of *According to Age* schools when year-groups have to be split.

Results

The results revealed a number of differences between schools organized by the *Traditional Standard* and *According to Age* methods.

A number of attainment tests were given to all the pupils in the selected sample schools. The results of these tests showed that where differences in the mean scores between the two types of school were significant, they were in favour of the *According to Age* schools. The consistency with which children from these schools performed better than their contemporaries in *Traditional Standard* schools varied from test to test. They scored significantly better on the English, Reading, Primary Verbal and Verbal tests, while on the Arithmetic tests, the scores again tended to favour pupils in the *According to Age* schools, but the differences between the two types of school were less often statistically significant.

It appeared that the superiority of the *According to Age* schools was due mainly to the fact that fewer pupils in these schools obtained very low scores; also, there was a trend for a larger number of pupils in *According to Age* than *Traditional Standard* schools to obtain high scores.

[1] The major disadvantages discussed in the report were that children who underwent accelerated promotion encountered problems of social and emotional adjustment by having to associate with older, more mature pupils; and those who failed to gain promotion suffered a loss of motivation which tended to give cause to disciplinary problems.

It was also found that the spread of scores (i.e. standard deviation) obtained in the *According to Age* schools was narrower than in *Traditional Standard* schools. Pupils in *According to Age* schools were more homogeneous with respect to attainment.

Demotion or retention of pupils with a younger year-group, the policy of *Traditional Standard* schools, does not appear to help the child's achievement scores; nor does promotion of brighter children appear to have any outstanding effects. It would appear that the overall effect of *Traditional Standard* policy is that it lowers the standards of the average and particularly the below average child.

In addition to achievements, a study was made of the psychological implications, as reflected in teacher ratings and sociometric data, of the two forms of organization.

No differences on the total maladjustment ratings were found, although on individual traits certain differences did emerge. For example, pupils from all social classes in *Traditional Standard* schools were considered by their teachers to be more prone to fighting and bullying, and the upper socio-economic group of pupils in *Traditional Standard* schools were rated more disobedient than their *According to Age* counterparts. On the other hand, pupils in the lower socio-economic group in *According to Age* schools were considered more withdrawn and less pleasurable to have in the class. But on the basis of sociometric data, classes in *According to Age* schools had a warmer and more friendly atmosphere.

Perhaps the children one would expect to be most affected by the school's policy are the 'demoted' and 'promoted' in the *Traditional Standard* schools and, in the *According to Age* schools, those who are separated from their year-group.

In the *Traditional Standard* schools, 'promoted' children were regarded by their teachers as more hardworking, more obedient, more pleasurable; whereas the 'demoted' were seen as lazier, less pleasurable, more prone to fighting, and more disobedient. Both promoted and demoted girls were prone to social isolation, as measured by sociometric choice; this was not the case for boys.

In the *According to Age* schools, on the other hand, no significant differences were found, in behaviour or maladjustment ratings, between 'younger' pupils 'kept down' or 'older' pupils 'put up', and the pupils in a class with their own year-group.

Demotion and promotion of pupils creates very heterogeneous classes in terms of ability and age.

The outcome of *Traditional Standard* policy is a class of children who are all roughly at about the same stage of educational development. However, as different standards of work are expected from different ages, some of the pupils in any one class can be described as bright, others average and still others dull, and the range of *standardized*

E

attainments (i.e. attainments relative to age-group) in any class will be as heterogeneous, one suspects, as that found in an *According to Age* class.

Moreover, the age-range is wide, and even though the conditions and size of the two types of school are similar, as many as 52 per cent of the *Traditional Standard* pupils compared with 26 per cent in *According to Age* schools, were in classes containing three or more year-groups. The outcome of this appears to be a lowering of standards of achievement.

It was found that 'demoted' children tended to be the youngest members of their year-group and 'promoted' children the oldest. Thus, at first glance there may be little to distinguish one type of school from the other, and in both there is a tendency for a similar pupil to be separated from the majority of his year-group. However, the difference would appear to be in the aura surrounding these pupils; teachers in *Traditional Standard* schools perceive the 'slower', demoted pupil as maladjusted, whereas pupils in the *According to Age* schools, when separated from their year-group, are perceived as normal.

This study does not permit one to draw conclusions concerning possible cause and effect relationships between factors affecting promotion and demotion, teachers' rating of ability and behaviour, and pupils' manifestation of disturbance or maladjustment. However, the characteristics found to be associated with the demoted child suggest that the *Traditional Standard* method creates or aggravates a problem both for the school and for the unfortunate pupils concerned.

A general finding of this study was that teachers, when estimating the ability of their pupils, made insufficient allowance for age difference. Consequently, the ability of the older children tended to be over-rated and the younger children under-rated. The teacher appears to judge her class as a whole and probably expects a certain standard of work which is based on the average of the class. The over- and under-estimating is very noticeable in a class of wide age-span. For example, in classes of three year-groups, the ability of the youngest year-group is the most under-estimated and the oldest year-group most over-estimated. Little research has been done on teacher expectancy and its effect on actual performance, but it is suggested that under-estimation of a child's ability could be self-fulfilling.

This tendency has also been noted in large schools where 'older' or winter-born children of a year-group tend to be allocated to 'A' streams and 'younger' or summer-born children to the lower streams.[1]

It would seem most important for teachers to be made aware of this, all too common, misjudgement.

[1] BARKER LUNN, J. C. (1967). 'The effects of streaming and non-streaming in junior schools: Second interim report', *New Research in Education*, vol. 1, pp. 46-75. (Distributed by NFER).

APPENDIX

Tables Not Included in the Text

TABLE A: *Significant Differences in Mean Scores on Tests between 'Traditional Standard' and 'According to Age' Schools*

Where the differences do not reach statistical significance, the letters AA and TS indicate that the trend is in favour of 'According to Age' or 'Traditional Standard' schools, respectively.

VERBAL				
Significance level				
		High Social Class	Low Social Class	All Social Classes
10+	Boys	5%	1%	1%
	Girls	AA	5%	5%
	Boys & Girls	5%	1%	0·1%

NON-VERBAL				
Significance level				
		High Social Class	Low Social Class	All Social Classes
10+	Boys	AA	AA	AA
	Girls	TS	AA	AA
	Boys & Girls	AA	AA	AA

Number of comparisons: 9.
Significant differences: 8 favour *According to Age* schools.
Non-significant differences in favour of *According to Age* schools: 1.

Number of comparisons: 9.
Non-significant differences in favour of *According to Age* schools: 8.
Non-significant differences in favour of *Traditional Standard* schools: 1.

PROBLEM ARITHMETIC					MECHANICAL ARITHMETIC			
Significance level					*Significance level*			
		High Social Class	Low Social Class	All Social Classes			High Social Class	Low Social Class	All Social Classes
7+	Boys	AA	AA	AA	7+	Boys	AA	AA	AA
	Girls	AA	AA	AA		Girls	TS	TS	TS
	Boys & Girls	AA	AA	AA		Boys & Girls	AA	AA	AA
8+	Boys	AA	TS	AA	8+	Boys	AA	TS	AA
	Girls	TS	AA	AA		Girls	TS	TS	TS
	Boys & Girls	AA	TS	AA		Boys & Girls	AA	TS	TS
9+	Boys	AA	TS	AA	9+	Boys	TS	TS	TS
	Girls	AA	AA	5%		Girls	AA	TS	AA
	Boys & Girls	AA	AA	AA		Boys & Girls	TS	TS	TS
10+	Boys	AA	AA	AA	10+	Boys	TS	AA	TS
	Girls	5%	AA	5%		Girls	AA	AA	AA
	Boys & Girls	AA	AA	5%		Boys & Girls	AA	AA	AA

Number of comparisons: 36.
Significant differences: 4 favour *According to Age* schools.
Non-significant differences in favour of *According to Age* schools: 28.
Non-significant differences in favour of *Traditional Standard* schools: 4.

Number of comparisons: 36.
Non-significant differences in favour of *According to Age* schools: 18.
Non-significant differences in favour of *Traditional Standard* schools: 18.

CONCEPT ARITHMETIC					PRIMARY VERBAL 1			
Significance level					*Significance level*			
		High Social Class	Low Social Class	All Social Classes			High Social Class	Low Social Class	All Social Classes
7+		Did not take test			7+		Did not take test		
8+	Boys	AA	TS	AA	8+	Boys	5%	AA	5%
	Girls	TS	TS	TS		Girls	AA	AA	AA
	Boys & Girls	AA	TS	TS		Boys & Girls	5%	5%	1%
9+	Boys	TS	TS	TS	9+	Boys	AA	AA	AA
	Girls	AA	AA	AA		Girls	AA	AA	5%
	Boys & Girls	AA	TS	TS		Boys & Girls	1%	AA	1%
10+	Boys	TS	TS	TS	10+	Boys	AA	AA	AA
	Girls	AA	AA	AA		Girls	AA	5%	1%
	Boys & Girls	AA	AA	AA		Boys & Girls	AA	1%	1%

Number of comparisons: 27.
Non-significant differences in favour of *According to Age* schools: 13.
Non-significant differences in favour of *Traditional Standard* schools: 14.

Number of comparisons: 27.
Significant differences: 12 favour *According to Age* schools.
Non-significant differences in favour of *According to Age* schools: 15.
Non-significant differences in favour of *Traditional Standard* schools: 0.

ENGLISH				
Significance level				
		High Social Class	Low Social Class	All Social Classes
7+	Boys	5%	5%	1%
	Girls	AA	5%	1%
	Boys & Girls	1%	1%	0·1%
8+	Boys	1%	AA	0·1%
	Girls	5%	AA	1%
	Boys & Girls	0·1%	5%	0·1%
9+	Boys	5%	AA	5%
	Girls	1%	5%	0·1%
	Boys & Girls	0·1%	5%	0·1%
10+	Boys	AA	5%	5%
	Girls	0·1%	5%	0·1%
	Boys & Girls	0·1%	1%	0·1%

READING				
Significance level				
		High Social Class	Low Social Class	All Social Classes
7+	Boys	5%	AA	AA
	Girls	AA	AA	AA
	Boys & Girls	AA	AA	5%
8+	Boys	AA	AA	AA
	Girls	AA	AA	AA
	Boys & Girls	5%	AA	5%
9+	Boys	AA	TS	AA
	Girls	AA	AA	5%
	Boys & Girls	5%	AA	AA
10+	Boys	TS	AA	AA
	Girls	AA	AA	5%
	Boys & Girls	AA	AA	AA

Number of comparisons: 36.
Significant differences: 31 favour *According to Age* schools.
Non-significant differences in favour of *According to Age* schools: 5.
Non-significant differences in favour of *Traditional Standard* schools: 0.

Number of comparisons: 36.
Significant differences: 7 favour *According to Age* schools.
Non-significant differences in favour of *According to Age* schools: 27.
Non-significant differences in favour of *Traditional Standard* schools: 2.

TABLE B: *Mean Scores and Standard Deviations for 'Traditional Standard' and 'According to Age' Schools*

		VERBAL—MEAN SCORES AND STANDARD DEVIATIONS										
		HIGH SOCIAL CLASS				LOW SOCIAL CLASS				ALL SOCIAL CLASSES			
		TS		AA		TS		AA		TS		AA	
		Mean	*SD*	*Mean*	*SD*	*Mean*	*SD*	*Mean*	*SD*	*Mean*	*SD*	*Mean*	*SD*
10+	Boys	24·73	8·85	27·60	8·19	18·95	9·35	22·96	8·58	21·99	9·54	25·21	8·71
	Girls	25·27	8·52	26·56	7·75	18·68	9·14	21·43	8·00	21·78	9·45	24·17	8·27
	Boys & Girls	24·96	8·72	27·02	7·96	18·82	9·25	22·18	8·32	21·89	9·50	24·65	8·49

		NON-VERBAL—MEAN SCORES AND STANDARD DEVIATIONS										
		HIGH SOCIAL CLASS				LOW SOCIAL CLASS				ALL SOCIAL CLASSES			
		TS		AA		TS		AA		TS		AA	
		Mean	*SD*	*Mean*	*SD*	*Mean*	*SD*	*Mean*	*SD*	*Mean*	*SD*	*Mean*	*SD*
10+	Boys	22·92	7·15	24·01	7·83	19·35	7·97	20·04	6·90	21·23	7·76	21·97	7·63
	Girls	23·00	6·40	22·91	6·14	18·18	7·49	19·05	6·60	20·44	7·40	21·11	6·64
	Boys & Girls	22·96	6·83	23·39	6·95	18·78	7·76	19·53	6·77	20·87	7·61	21·51	7·13

		PROBLEM ARITHMETIC—MEAN SCORES AND STANDARD DEVIATIONS											
		HIGH SOCIAL CLASS				LOW SOCIAL CLASS				ALL SOCIAL CLASSES			
		TS		AA		TS		AA		TS		AA	
		Mean	*SD*	*Mean*	*SD*	*Mean*	*SD*	*Mean*	*SD*	*Mean*	*SD*	*Mean*	*SD*
7+	Boys	12·07	7·34	12·38	6·37	9·23	5·32	9·87	5·57	11·00	6·79	11·32	6·17
	Girls	10·27	6·24	10·98	6·64	7·80	5·59	9·07	5·79	9·01	6·04	10·05	6·31
	Boys & Girls	11·28	6·93	11·71	6·54	8·40	5·52	9·43	5·71	10·00	6·50	10·67	6·28
8+	Boys	16·51	8·38	18·46	7·49	14·35	7·00	13·29	7·01	15·40	7·78	15·75	7·69
	Girls	17·07	8·04	17·03	8·11	12·82	7·78	13·86	6·84	15·23	8·20	15·54	7·71
	Boys & Girls	16·81	8·20	17·65	7·88	13·64	7·41	13·58	6·93	15·31	8·00	15·64	7·70
9+	Boys	25·18	10·77	25·88	10·04	20·84	10·20	20·17	8·61	23·09	10·72	23·17	9·81
	Girls	22·32	9·24	24·74	9·10	17·80	9·41	20·18	9·47	19·73	9·60	22·18	9·58
	Boys & Girls	23·85	10·19	25·34	9·63	19·15	9·89	20·17	9·10	21·36	10·30	22·66	9·70
10+	Boys	30·79	9·60	31·78	8·96	24·80	11·09	26·36	9·10	27·91	10·77	29·05	9·43
	Girls	26·28	9·31	29·91	9·71	23·36	11·49	24·67	10·17	24·72	10·64	27·51	10·26
	Boys & Girls	28·83	9·74	30·76	9·43	24·10	11·31	25·51	9·69	26·44	10·83	28·24	9·91

TABLE B: *continued*

		High Social Class				Low Social Class				All Social Classes			
		TS		AA		TS		AA		TS		AA	
		Mean	SD	Mean	SD	Mean	SD	Mean	SD	Mean	SD	Mean	SD
7+	Boys	9·04	5·83	9·64	5·01	6·15	4·55	6·65	4·00	7·92	5·55	8·26	4·81
	Girls	7·95	5·12	7·86	5·54	6·34	4·14	6·14	4·28	7·14	4·72	7·00	5·02
	Boys & Girls	8·55	5·55	8·78	5·35	6·26	4·33	6·39	4·15	7·54	5·17	7·63	4·96
8+	Boys	12·95	7·03	14·18	6·39	9·98	5·09	9·04	5·09	11·39	6·26	11·81	6·25
	Girls	13·96	5·92	13·53	5·38	11·07	6·16	10·74	5·40	12·71	6·19	12·23	5·57
	Boys & Girls	13·49	6·46	13·83	5·87	10·47	5·62	10·10	5·29	12·04	6·26	12·03	5·90
9+	Boys	18·65	6·87	17·56	6·65	15·78	7·13	14·48	6·99	17·33	7·14	16·17	6·98
	Girls	17·14	7·45	18·38	6·17	14·34	6·16	13·79	6·58	15·57	6·90	15·76	6·80
	Boys & Girls	17·98	7·17	17·92	6·45	14·99	6·66	14·09	6·77	16·46	7·08	15·96	6·89
10+	Boys	22·10	5·85	22·01	5·71	18·77	7·42	18·79	5·91	20·50	6·85	20·36	6·03
	Girls	21·03	6·38	21·61	6·26	17·19	7·02	18·37	6·49	18·99	7·00	20·14	6·57
	Boys & Girls	21·63	6·11	21·80	6·02	18·01	7·27	18·59	6·20	19·81	6·96	20·25	6·32

Mechanical Arithmetic—Mean scores and standard deviations

CONCEPT ARITHMETIC—MEAN SCORES AND STANDARD DEVIATIONS											
		HIGH SOCIAL CLASS				LOW SOCIAL CLASS				ALL SOCIAL CLASSES			
		TS		AA		TS		AA		TS		AA	
		Mean	*SD*	*Mean*	*SD*	*Mean*	*SD*	*Mean*	*SD*	*Mean*	*SD*	*Mean*	*SD*
8+	Boys	20·03	12·81	21·35	10·96	14·84	8·70	14·28	9·59	17·31	11·16	17·74	10·87
	Girls	20·59	10·88	19·71	10·60	15·64	10·12	15·34	6·99	18·37	10·83	17·62	9·30
	Boys & Girls	20·33	11·82	20·46	10·80	15·21	9·39	14·82	8·37	17·84	11·01	17·68	10·08
9+	Boys	29·40	13·31	29·05	13·72	25·28	13·70	21·98	12·94	27·51	13·65	25·77	13·82
	Girls	27·70	13·80	29·84	11·22	20·74	11·06	21·59	11·19	23·83	12·82	25·08	11·92
	Boys & Girls	28·65	13·55	29·45	12·66	22·84	12·55	21·76	11·98	25·70	13·38	25·42	12·89
10+	Boys	36·00	12·49	35·88	12·61	29·49	14·27	29·24	10·43	32·89	13·76	32·49	12·01
	Girls	34·32	13·38	37·13	12·93	26·54	13·51	28·19	11·34	30·23	14·00	33·25	13·04
	Boys & Girls	35·25	12·92	36·57	12·80	28·04	13·98	28·74	10·88	31·65	13·93	32·89	12·56

PRIMARY VERBAL—MEAN SCORES AND STANDARD DEVIATIONS											
		HIGH SOCIAL CLASS				LOW SOCIAL CLASS				ALL SOCIAL CLASSES			
		TS		AA		TS		AA		TS		AA	
		Mean	*SD*	*Mean*	*SD*	*Mean*	*SD*	*Mean*	*SD*	*Mean*	*SD*	*Mean*	*SD*
8+	Boys	45·06	22·23	52·69	19·44	36·85	18·88	41·15	18·61	40·85	20·99	46·88	19·88
	Girls	47·99	19·26	51·82	20·03	34·41	21·86	39·57	19·51	42·17	21·49	46·02	20·71
	Boys & Girls	46·62	20·75	52·21	19·77	35·76	20·31	40·33	19·10	41·50	21·25	46·42	20·34
9+	Boys	59·46	20·61	64·77	15·78	53·85	20·05	55·45	18·42	56·83	20·54	60·52	17·65
	Girls	58·47	19·92	64·43	14·42	46·02	21·55	49·79	18·50	51·26	21·77	56·09	18·36
	Boys & Girls	59·02	20·31	64·62	15·19	49·54	21·25	52·27	18·68	54·06	21·34	58·28	18·15
10+	Boys	70·05	14·47	71·31	12·56	57·15	21·80	62·82	16·61	63·93	19·42	66·98	15·36
	Girls	66·83	17·71	71·21	12·17	55·56	20·14	61·72	16·83	60·86	19·85	66·79	15·28
	Boys & Girls	68·66	16·03	71·25	12·34	56·38	21·02	62·26	16·73	62·52	19·68	66·88	15·32

TABLE B: *continued*

		ENGLISH—MEAN SCORES AND STANDARD DEVIATIONS											
		HIGH SOCIAL CLASS				LOW SOCIAL CLASS				ALL SOCIAL CLASSES			
		TS		AA		TS		AA		TS		AA	
		Mean	SD	Mean	SD	Mean	SD	Mean	SD	Mean	SD	Mean	SD
7+	Boys	16·26	13·65	20·77	12·91	9·17	10·61	13·18	11·07	13·53	13·03	17·24	12·67
	Girls	14·51	11·69	17·93	13·39	9·40	9·19	12·85	10·73	11·92	10·80	15·39	12·40
	Boys & Girls	15·48	12·84	19·41	13·22	9·30	9·83	13·01	10·90	12·72	11·99	16·32	12·57
8+	Boys	24·08	16·47	32·82	16·01	18·04	13·51	21·58	14·73	20·93	15·30	27·09	16·37
	Girls	26·44	16·01	32·65	16·18	18·18	15·60	21·83	15·05	22·86	16·35	27·58	16·57
	Boys & Girls	25·34	16·27	32·73	16·11	18·10	14·48	21·71	14·90	21·88	15·86	27·35	16·48
9+	Boys	35·92	16·95	42·43	15·13	30·90	17·44	33·86	17·16	33·61	17·36	38·54	16·64
	Girls	35·32	17·77	43·57	14·49	25·52	16·28	31·68	15·97	29·82	17·64	36·83	16·44
	Boys & Girls	35·65	17·33	42·95	14·85	27·97	17·03	32·62	16·53	31·73	17·60	37·66	16·56
10+	Boys	45·45	13·98	49·41	11·20	36·88	17·98	42·44	14·50	41·26	16·62	45·78	13·48
	Girls	41·35	16·09	50·11	12·49	33·16	17·93	40·25	14·38	37·01	17·57	45·64	14·25
	Boys & Girls	43·63	15·09	49·80	11·95	35·08	18·05	41·36	14·48	39·29	17·20	45·70	13·89

		READING—MEAN SCORES AND STANDARD DEVIATIONS											
		HIGH SOCIAL CLASS				LOW SOCIAL CLASS				ALL SOCIAL CLASSES			
		TS		AA		TS		AA		TS		AA	
		Mean	*SD*	*Mean*	*SD*	*Mean*	*SD*	*Mean*	*SD*	*Mean*	*SD*	*Mean*	*SD*
7+	Boys	18·14	9·11	20·55	7·16	12·95	8·61	15·05	8·01	16·19	9·27	18·02	8·04
	Girls	17·33	8·92	18·40	8·36	12·77	8·51	13·67	7·64	14·94	9·00	16·05	8·35
	Boys & Girls	17·79	9·04	19·55	7·81	12·85	8·55	14·36	7·85	15·57	9·16	17·07	8·25
8+	Boys	23·57	10·42	26·04	8·83	19·17	8·03	19·54	8·71	21·33	9·54	22·79	9·35
	Girls	23·43	8·97	25·20	7·60	17·28	10·54	19·22	8·49	20·75	10·15	22·39	8·57
	Boys & Girls	23·50	9·68	25·59	8·20	18·30	9·31	19·37	8·60	21·04	9·85	22·58	8·95
9+	Boys	29·81	9·58	31·51	8·13	26·07	9·04	25·99	8·78	28·11	9·52	28·96	8·89
	Girls	28·55	9·15	31·11	7·77	22·72	10·25	24·47	7·49	25·22	10·21	27·35	8·29
	Boys & Girls	29·27	9·42	31·33	7·99	24·25	9·86	25·14	8·12	26·70	9·97	28·14	8·63
10+	Boys	34·49	8·26	34·35	6·59	29·71	10·44	30·29	8·21	32·21	9·67	32·29	7·72
	Girls	32·54	10·43	34·20	6·12	26·90	10·24	29·12	8·01	29·52	10·70	31·86	7·50
	Boys & Girls	33·64	9·32	34·27	6·34	28·33	10·44	29·70	8·13	30·96	10·25	32·07	7·61

TABLE C: *Significant Differences in Standard Deviation of Test Scores between 'Traditional Standard' and 'According to Age' Schools*

It is evident from the following tables that by far the greater number of significant differences in spread of score occurs at the 10+ level. Where the difference does not reach statistical significance, the letters AA or TS indicate that the trend is in favour of *According to Age* or *Traditional Standard* schools respectively.

Where the difference is significant, this means that the spread of score was narrower in the *According to Age* school. The letters AA or TS indicate that the trend was towards a narrower range of score in that particular type of school.

7+ PUPILS									
	High Social Class			Low Social Class			All Social Classes		
	Boys	*Girls*	*Boys & Girls*	*Boys*	*Girls*	*Boys & Girls*	*Boys*	*Girls*	*Boys & Girls*
Reading	5%	AA	AA	AA	AA	AA	AA	AA	AA
English	AA	TS	TS	TS	TS	TS	AA	TS	TS
Mechanical Arithmetic	AA	TS	AA	AA	TS	AA	AA	TS	AA
Problem Arithmetic	AA	TS	AA	TS	TS	TS	AA	TS	AA

8+ PUPILS									
	High Social Class			Low Social Class			All Social Classes		
	Boys	*Girls*	*Boys & Girls*	*Boys*	*Girls*	*Boys & Girls*	*Boys*	*Girls*	*Boys & Girls*
Reading	AA	AA	AA	TS	5%	AA	AA	5%	AA
English	AA	TS	AA	TS	AA	TS	TS	TS	TS
Mechanical Arithmetic	AA	AA	AA	†	AA	AA	AA	AA	AA
Problem Arithmetic	AA	TS	AA	TS	AA	AA	AA	AA	AA
Concept Arithmetic	AA	AA	AA	TS	5%	AA	AA	AA	AA
Primary Verbal	AA	TS	AA	AA	AA	AA	AA	AA	AA

† Standard deviation the same.

9+ Pupils									
	High Social Class			Low Social Class			All Social Classes		
	Boys	*Girls*	*Boys & Girls*	*Boys*	*Girls*	*Boys & Girls*	*Boys*	*Girls*	*Boys & Girls*
Reading	AA	AA	AA	AA	1%	AA	AA	5%	AA
English	AA	AA	AA	AA	AA	AA	AA	AA	AA
Mechanical Arithmetic	AA	AA	AA	AA	TS	TS	AA	AA	AA
Problem Arithmetic	AA	AA	AA	AA	TS	AA	AA	AA	AA
Concept Arithmetic	TS	5%	AA	AA	TS	AA	TS	AA	AA
Primary Verbal	1%	1%	1%	AA	AA	AA	AA	AA	AA

10+ Pupils									
	High Social Class			Low Social Class			All Social Classes		
	Boys	*Girls*	*Boys & Girls*	*Boys*	*Girls*	*Boys & Girls*	*Boys*	*Girls*	*Boys & Girls*
Reading	5%	0·1%	0·1%	5%	5%	5%	1%	0·1%	0·1%
English	5%	5%	5%	5%	5%	1%	1%	1%	1%
Mechanical Arithmetic	AA	AA	AA	5%	AA	AA	AA	AA	AA
Problem Arithmetic	AA	TS	AA	AA	AA	AA	AA	AA	AA
Concept Arithmetic	TS	AA	AA	1%	5%	1%	AA	AA	AA
Primary Verbal	AA	0·1%	1%	1%	5%	1%	1%	1%	1%
Verbal	AA	AA	AA	AA	AA	AA	AA	AA	AA
Non-Verbal	TS	AA	TS	AA	AA	AA	AA	AA	AA